Surviving a d
... on a Shoestring

Building a successful business ...
without breaking the bank

Jeremy Kourdi

BLOOMSBURY

First published in Great Britain 2007 by A & C Black Publishers Ltd

This edition first published 2011

Bloomsbury Publishing Plc
50 Bedford Square, London WC1B 3PD

British Library Cataloguing in Publication Data

A CIP record for this book is available from the British Library.

ISBN: 978-1-4081-3986-8

This book is produced using paper that is made from wood grown in managed, sustainable forests. It is natural, renewable and recyclable. The logging and manufacturing processes conform to the environmental regulations of the country of origin.

Design by Fiona Pike, Pike Design, Winchester
Typeset by RefineCatch Limited, Bungay, Suffolk
Printed and bound by CPI Group (UK) Ltd, Croydon, CR0 4YY

CONTENTS

Introduction   vii
Acknowledgements   ix

1. What causes a business downturn?   1
2. Practical techniques for boosting profitability   25
3. Focusing on customers   54
4. Increasing revenue: marketing and pricing   68
5. Improving sales and the sales process   88
6. Controlling costs and cash flow   109
7. Leading your business through a downturn   122
8. Leading your team during tough times   143
9. Making decisions and solving problems   159

Index   171

INTRODUCTION

In business, a downturn is never more than a few minutes away. Major customers can leave, disappear or refuse to pay; your brand can be damaged, fairly or unfairly, by ignorance or malice. Mistakes, acts of God or simple actions and unforeseen sequences of events can all conspire to create adversity.

The fact is that the best businesses are those that are energetic, thoughtful and restless, and that avoid complacency, are continuously learning, adapting and improving—in short, even if a downturn is not present, the best businesses act as if one is right around the corner and there is no time to waste. In a fast-moving, competitive global economy, this seems to be a sound approach to ensuring success.

Surviving a downturn is one of the hardest and most challenging tasks in business. Downturns can result from a range of factors, including economic shifts, external market changes, competitive pressures or simple mismanagement. While people tend to focus on immediate problems that cause an enterprise to fail, such as a lack of cash or sales problems, these may actually mask a range of business issues that result in failure. Such issues can include weak leadership, a lack of market awareness, poor use of information and an inability to innovate. The solutions to surviving a downturn or 'competitive squeeze' are therefore not simply financial or sales-focused, but much broader, covering the long and the short term, and they provide the focus for this book.

These issues affect the largest corporations as well as the smallest enterprises, so this book is illustrated with examples relevant to a diverse set of challenges: focusing on customers, controlling the money, thinking ahead, building trust, being creative, getting the right plan and working with people to succeed.

Whether you are surviving a current downturn or simply avoiding a future one, I hope this book will help you and your business to find firm ground, providing ideas and insights that ensure you prosper.

Jeremy Kourdi

ACKNOWLEDGEMENTS

This book is the result of the active support of two people and whilst the execution, style and shortcomings are my own, their expertise and help must certainly be acknowledged. First, my business partner and son, Thomas Kourdi, whose diligence is much appreciated and who has been a valuable source of information and well-informed opinion. Second, my editor at Bloomsbury, Lisa Carden, who suggested the idea for the book and provided patient encouragement.

Finally, my gratitude goes, as always, to my wife, Julie, and daughter, Louise, for their constant support and the inspiration to write.

1

WHAT CAUSES A BUSINESS DOWNTURN?

The most simple but possibly alarming answer to this question is – you. Of course, this is both bad news and good. It's bad because the potential for a downturn in business success is always there, but it's also particularly good news as well. If the only potential pitfall is one that you know intimately and can control, then your chances of surviving a downturn are greatly increased.

The view that you are the potential pitfall is one that seems counter-intuitive. What about the myriad other things that decisively affect your business that you cannot control: customers' cash flow, competitors' products and pricing, the strength of the economy, legislation, unforeseen developments affecting your market, employees' fraud? The list is almost endless. Surely these are the real causes of business failure or success?

Well, these are certainly the factors behind business fortunes, but they're not the most significant when trying to survive a downturn. The truth is that you can't control the world, you can't control the market (regulators will prevent that), nor your customers or even the people who work in your business. While you may be able to influence all of these forces, the only one you truly *control* is yourself.

When you're facing a downturn, you need to be aware of both the challenges and opportunities facing your business, and you need to reflect that understanding by taking decisions at the right time. To illustrate, consider the case of Gary Flandro.

During the mid-1960s Flandro was an undergraduate student on a work placement with the NASA space agency. At that time NASA was in the middle of the first Mariner missions to Mars, and Flandro was given the routine and (supposedly) far less interesting task of calculating, in detail, the movement and relative positions of the planets and the best time to launch a probe for a future expedition to Jupiter.

Flandro approached the task carefully and enthusiastically. He understood that the gravitational field of one planet could slingshot a probe on to another target at even greater speed, and he calculated when the four largest planets in the solar system would be on the same side of the sun, in the same proximity. He then calculated that a specific timing for a mission to Jupiter would, because of their proximity, also enable the probe to visit Saturn, Uranus and Neptune. Finally, Flandro worked out that only once every 175 years were the four planets close enough to make such a mission viable. This led NASA during the 1970s and 1980s to launch the enormously successful Pioneer and Voyager space probes, that dramatically increased our understanding of the solar system (Voyager is now the most distant and far travelled object in human history). Not bad for a young student given a routine task to complete!

So what does Gary Flandro have to do with our understanding of the causes of a business downturn? One point is worth noting at the outset: Flandro highlights the fact that inspiration and insight can come from anywhere—home, family, friends, public service, academia—not just business. More particularly, Flandro's success shows that it's what we do with the information around us that determines success or failure, not the information itself. Understanding the movement and position of the planets was not Flandro's great achievement—this had been studied in a rudimentary way since ancient times. His great success was to build on this understanding and realise its implications (the chance for a slingshot mission once every 175 years). Events may be challenging but it's our *response* that determines success.

We'll discuss in detail how to avoid and survive a business downturn later, but for now, there's one vital lesson. Surviving a business downturn means taking 100% responsibility for your business and its results. And this means not blaming, complaining, justifying, defending or withdrawing, but becoming actively involved, focusing your thinking and applying the skills and abilities you have to get the business out of its tailspin. As the business philosopher Jim Rohn noted, 'You must take personal responsibility. You cannot change the circumstances, the seasons or the wind, but you can change yourself.'

To highlight *how* to take 100% responsibility, consider the formula

$$E + R = O$$
(Event + Response = Outcome)

To achieve a specific outcome, you need to take control of your reactions. Being able to influence events would help, but clearly this is not always possible; what is achievable, however, is a positive, productive response leading to the right outcome.

The basic premise is that every outcome you experience in your life is the result of how you have responded to an earlier event or events. If you want to improve the results you are getting, then you can simply change your response (R) to the events (E)—the way things are—until you achieve the outcome (O) that you want. To control your response, focus on three specific elements within your control: behaviour, thoughts and images.

Changing your response requires a change in attitude, but it helps to know that for most people a large proportion of their behaviour (85–90%) is habitual and unconscious. Simply managing this aspect of behaviour will make a significant difference. After all, your current habits will get you only as far as you are at the moment. What is needed is the ability to adopt—or sustain—the right mindset.

There is one final, positive point to note. Reversing the causes of a downturn results in real progress and success, not simply 'an end to the rot' but something much more positive. In business you are either going forwards or backwards, but never static. You may think you're standing still—for example, this year's results may look very similar to last year's—but in fact your long-term prospects could be declining and you could be entering a downturn. So, don't think of surviving a downturn as being defensive, defeatist or essentially negative: it's entirely about making progress and achieving commercial success.

Challenge 1: adopt the right mindset

How can you make sure that you have the right mindset to overcome the challenges of surviving a downturn? Or, if you like to think of the glass as half empty rather than half full, how do you know when your approach is causing a problem for your business, and what can you do about it? The answer will, of course, be very different from business to business, but there are several fundamental steps that every company can benefit from.

Believe in yourself

Focus your energies on what you're good at and strive to improve your abilities in those essential areas where there is a clear, identifiable benefit. In particular, don't think that you're 'weak'. Believe in yourself and your abilities. It really does matter, for several reasons:

- **we're stronger and more capable when we think positively than when we think negatively**
- **you'll waste both time and effort if you don't believe your can achieve your goal**
- **it encourages energy, clarity, focus and persistence—and many other attributes that will enable you to succeed**
- **you have to believe in yourself even when no one else does. You don't need all the right answers but you do need the right attitude: a positive approach focused on making your goals happen.**

Even though you may be going through a tough time at the moment, don't forget all your past successes: how did you achieve them? Are there any lessons or tactics you can carry across to help combat your present situation? Finally, there are some things that just can't be delegated or ignored. If you want to succeed, you'll have to pull out all the stops and put in as much effort as possible yourself.

Decide what you want—and set goals to help you get there

In the bestseller *Good to Great*, business author Jim Collins highlights the significance of goal-setting. The best executives establish 'Big, Hairy, Audacious Goals'—stretching, challenging goals that inspire and motivate people, bringing out their best qualities. Goals are especially valuable as they help to provide clarity and focus. In addition, your goals should be measurable.

Start by deciding exactly what you want. Create a vision in your own mind of how things will be when success is attained: visions can be very powerful motivators that can help you keep your activities on track. Next, establish those clear, stretching goals that will drive your progress along the way. The process of achieving a stretching goal is itself virtuous, making you more likely to succeed, irrespective of the goal itself. Anecdotal research suggests that less than 10% of people have personal goals.

Focus on breakthrough goals, those achievements that will take your success to a new level, further and faster than might otherwise be attained. Also, everyday, at least twice a day, focus on your goals: this is because what you think about is much more likely to come about.

Practise the 'rule of five'

Once you've clearly defined a set of goals that are challenging and personal to you, do five things each day that will help you to achieve them. This 'to-do' list will help you focus the way you think and the actions you take.

Stop complaining, and work with successful people

This links closely with the earlier need to believe in oneself and be positive and to take 100% responsibility. Complaining can become a habit: we become so used to complaining that it can be very difficult to stop. The reason it is so important to knock it on the head is because it just gets in the way of our ability to respond effectively to situations, challenges and opportunities. We get too focused on what went wrong, why it went wrong and its consequences, rather than taking a productive approach of finding a successful way forward.

One way to stop complaining is simple: avoid people who complain, as their attitude easily spreads. The converse is also true: if you surround yourself with positive people, you're much more likely to take on the attitudes, values and energy that have helped to make them successful, and by moving in the circles of successful people you are more likely to achieve your goals. This is because whether consciously or unconsciously, many high achievers recognise in others the qualities that achieve success. They may provide support, guidance, practical help or, at the very least, motivation and encouragement.

Self-awareness and developing the right personal mindset are vital. Without them, a business (and personal) downturn is more likely; *with* them, on the other hand, success is more assured.

Challenge 2: stop being complacent, too focused on short-term goals or simply unaware

Some of the commercial causes of a downturn are obvious: for example, your business might not have the right product or price; you might not have enough customers; your product might not be in the right place at the right time; or you might not be able to reach your customers and persuade them to buy from you. To get through this variety of issues, though, you need to have good information in a timely fashion so that you can take and implement the best possible decisions.

Develop your commercial awareness

Being up to speed with commercial trends is one good way of avoiding a business slump. Highlighting this point is the example of Foster Brothers—a mens' casualwear retailer—which owned shops on most UK high streets in the 1970s. One year, sales began to decline and they responded by using the traditional success formula of cost-effective procurement of finished goods—for them, this meant sourcing cheaper supplies of menswear made to Foster Brothers' own designs. Over the next few years, the company reapplied this recipe many times and the well-made items of menswear sold at very competitive prices. Foster Brothers maintained its margins on the basis of its excellent procurement process.

However, the success proved to be temporary, and in time Foster Brothers went out of business. The reasons for this failure can be traced back to the inertia evident in their strategic thinking. Men in the UK had become fashion conscious and preferred to shop at other emerging retailers more in tune with men's current fashion trends and style. In short, Foster Brothers' success formula no longer matched what their customers wanted. An aspect of their business environment had changed in a way that Foster Brothers seemed unable to appreciate.

Use knowledge and information

Being able to find and use the right information in the right way is at the heart of commercial awareness, as we explore in more detail in Chapter 3. However, it's worth appreciating that, for now, what matters is a business's collective skills and knowledge, and how they are managed. Businesses succeed because they have scarcity: they provide something that is distinctive, meaning more convenient or more valuable than their competitors can provide or something that is simply unique. Central to achieving this is knowledge. Thomas Stewart, author of the book *Intellectual Capital*, commented: 'Knowledge has become the most important factor in economic life. It is the chief ingredient of what we buy and sell, the raw materials with which we work. Intellectual capital—not natural resources, machinery or even financial capital—has become the one indispensable asset of corporations.'

The rising importance of knowledge suggests that, to be successful, a business will need to be what's known as a 'learning organisation', an enterprise that is constantly sensing, valuing and sharing information, and using this information flexibly to improve efficiency, generate profitable new ideas and, above all, to add value for customers.

Avoid 'business as usual' thinking

Many businesses fail because they get stuck in a rut as Foster Brothers did. They allow their success 'recipes' to become routines that guide the way they think and act. If your business is to survive, though, it's essential that the decisions it takes match up with what external world wants. In other words, don't follow recipes just because you always have before; be ready to change them if they're no longer appropriate.

Sometimes, though, strategic inertia takes over and people are reluctant to change the way they do things in any way other than incrementally. There is a danger here: just as your business reacts to the outside world slowly, you'll gradually become distanced from it, sometimes almost imperceptibly, like being cut off from the mainland at high tide.

'Business as usual' thinking:

- prevents managers from sensing problems
- delays changes in strategy and tactics
- leads to action that has no connection to your customers or the real world

Focusing on the wrong priorities or being complacent can happen to any size of business at any time, and this can be fatal. A classic example of flawed thinking and lack of awareness is provided by Xerox, who in the early 1970s held a 95% market share of the global copier industry. Their target customers were large corporations and their concept of customer value was that of centrally controlled photocopying. Xerox focused on manufacturing and leasing complex high-speed photocopiers, using its own manufacturing and sales service force to provide a complete package to those who leased its machines. The firm's name became so synonymous with this everyday office task that people did not copy documents, they 'Xeroxed' them.

Viewed over a 35-year period, the story of Xerox's business fortunes is a remarkable rollercoaster ride of fabulous highs and terrifying lows. We follow its story into the 21st century in Chapter 7.

Challenge 3: decide and then implement the right approach

Linked with the need for awareness, urgency and an absence of complacency is the ability to do the right things, in the right way at the right time. In other words, you need to get things done with making mistakes en route. (Turn to Chapter 9 for advice on the essentials of decision making under pressure.)

For now, it is useful to highlight several points about the causes of a downturn from interesting research highlighting the problems for organisations that are unable to detect or respond to change (known as the Sharpbenders' research). The research concentrated on companies that had been failing, as shown by a stock value that had been slipping against the market average, but that had been able to turn things around. That is where the word *sharpbenders* came from—a slipping stock value followed by a recovery. The idea was that these companies, having been able to turn things around, would be able to articulate what had gone wrong and why this had happened. After all, if they managed to turn things around they must have made a successful diagnosis of what went on during the downward period of their history.

Having identified such companies from stock market records, the researchers interviewed many of them and produced a list of what can go wrong (see Grinyer, Mayes and McKiernan, *Sharpbenders: The Secrets of Unleashing Corporate Potential*, Blackwell, 1989). The findings identify five key causes of decline:

1. **adverse development in market demand or increased competition**
2. **high cost structure**
3. **poor financial controls**
4. **failure of big projects**
5. **acquisition problems**

Interesting though these are, Sharpbenders was significant because the causes of failure that they identified can be divided into two categories: 'hygiene factors' and 'business idea factors'. Surviving a downturn means understanding the difference between the two.

Differentiate between 'hygiene factors' and the business idea

Businesses have always tried to find ways of outsmarting the competition. Not all ideas are equally effective, but some stand out as clearly successful. Initially, some organisations develop significant competitive advantage by exploiting these ideas, but, over time, others see the beneficial effects and start to copy the same ideas in their own organisations. Eventually, some of these approaches become so popular that they're used by the best companies in the world, noted in textbooks and taught to others. Once an idea reaches this point, it has become a 'hygiene factor'— something that is generally recognised as fundamental in running any healthy organisation. Businesses without hygiene factors, are, essentially, non-starters.

Most hygiene factors are about the need to have efficient business processes, which make sure that a company remains a going concern. These processes are the generally accepted basics for running any organisation; they are qualifiers, allowing you to play the game. *Winning* the game, however, requires much more: additional, distinctive factors and capabilities that will distinguish the winner from the loser.

Get the business idea right

When you're trying to judge the strength of a business idea, think about these three fundamental factors.

1. **The idea must be able to explain how value will be created.** No business can survive without creating value. We know that value is being created if the business addresses a scarcity somewhere, either by filling it or by alleviating its effect. This is what moves customers to come to you to buy your products.

2. **It must have something unique to offer.** If there is nothing unique in what the organisation does, it won't be engaging in any unique activities and as a result, doesn't address any scarcity. A business idea has to be very clear about the uniqueness that the organisation brings to its activities.

3. It must develop to survive. Once an organisation makes a unique contribution and creates value, it can charge a price for its efforts and so generate new resources to continue its growth. However, a success formula can't be effective for ever. Anything that is unique will eventually be copied and if people's interest moves elsewhere (as is likely), its value may disappear. Therefore, an organisation must be able to show how its approach can be developed, sustaining its distinctiveness.

These three factors work together in a loop that supports itself and strengthens the firm.

Find, agree and implement the best strategy

Running a thriving business is about making choices and then moving the firm in the direction that has been decided. The Sharpbenders' research highlighted several strategic reasons for business failure:

* failure to identify a clear direction and a lack of recognisable strategies and policies
* poor execution or timing of responses to developments such as declining demand or increasing competition
* inappropriate risk taking in projects that are too big for the business undertaking them on, or excessive optimism

Find your own way out of the downturn

There is some good news, however! The Sharpbenders' research findings showed that a decline in organisational performance can be halted if business owners or managers:

- **understand and meet the changing needs of their customers**
- **ensure a strong sales culture**
- **instill a clear product focus that concentrates on what the firm does best**
- **regularly review strategy (the bigger the business grows, the more likely it is that this process will become very formal)**

In short, get the right route to market with the right offer, and, at the same time, adopt a forward-looking approach which invests in the future.

Manage your hygiene factors

As noted above, if your business doesn't have the right hygiene factors, it's going to struggle. Some common issues include:

- **poor cash management.** Often, areas such as credit, working capital, budgets, costs, cash flow and quality aren't given the attention they need. This is frequently due to inadequate management information, leading to infrequent or incomplete reports that are late, too complex, irrelevant or erroneous.
- **a poor management style.** There are as many management styles are there are people, but there are common pitfalls you can avoid: make sure you're flexible, that you delegate well and that you're not over-cautious.
- **failure to communicate purpose and the business idea.** This can happen between the top and middle management and between management and the work

force. In a small business, it's likely that you're working with a relatively compact team, so regularly take time to get across what you're all working towards.

■ **a weakness in maintaining sound and efficient relationships with 'stakeholders',** and as a result failing to sense or respond to external change. Maintaining relationships with stakeholders—such as shareholders, suppliers and customers—is essential, as any of these groups has the power to threaten an organisation's very existence. Shareholders can decide to invest elsewhere; customers may 'vote with their feet'; governments can pass unfavourable legislation; and so on. These vital groups have to be kept on board. Their conflicting expectations need to be identified and reconciled.

I would argue that each of these issues is not only a competitive *necessity*, but also a potential source of competitive advantage. We'll explore these issues in later chapters precisely because they are responsible for many firms going into a downturn and out of business, and because they lie on the road to survival and progress.

Challenge 4: develop creativity and innovation
As Xerox and Foster Brothers showed, firms that forget how to innovate will decline and disappear. Creativity and innovation give businesses the flexibility to meet customers' needs and allow them to adapt to shifting external conditions. These skills increase competitiveness, enabling the firm to exercise greater control over its business environment.

Despite this, it's only recently that the creative talent of people at work has been seen as a major asset that needs to be unlocked. This realisation has highlighted two aspects of creativity and innovation. Firstly, everyone has the capacity for creativity—outside work, individuals can be hugely creative. Indeed, to be fully motivated and achieve success, people often need to realise their creative potential. Secondly, organisations increasingly require creativity and innovation for success, not simply to keep up with the rapid pace of change, competition and new opportunities, but also to solve problems and to make the best decisions.

EasyJet, the low-cost airline operating a business model similar to Southwest Airlines in the US, is a great example of how using creativity can build a small business into a major success. EasyJet's success came at a time when the global airline industry was reeling from the double-whammy of increased costs and static or declining passenger numbers. As even the relentlessly entrepreneurial Richard Branson put it, 'The safest way to become a millionaire is to start as a billionaire and invest in the airline industry'.

Stelios Haji-Ioannou, who, at the time he launched EasyJet in November 1995 was a 32-year-old with little experience of the airline business, followed another low-fare European operator, Ryanair, in challenging the entire industry. He focused on creating a very efficient operating system, building brand awareness and maintaining high levels of customer satisfaction—factors that would reinforce each other and ensure that EasyJet was distinctive. In Haji-Ioannou's view: 'If you create the right expectations, and you meet or exceed those expectations, then you will have happy customers'.

EasyJet's operation was similar to the model originally developed by Southwest Airlines, which provided short-haul travel in one type of aircraft (Boeing 737s), with no in-flight meals, and a rapid turnaround time resulting in aircraft utilisation up to 50% greater than the industry average. EasyJet took this approach further, completely avoiding travel agents, not issuing tickets, selling food and drink on the plane, and building sales through the Internet.

Also, EasyJet's founders sought from day one to reduce bureaucracy and hierarchy as much as possible. For example, apart from payroll details, all information within the company is openly available. All mail, memos, business plans and sales data are scanned and are accessible to the whole organisation. EasyJet's marketing director has a direct telephone line and no secretary to field calls, achieving the dual benefits of reducing costs and being in constant, direct touch with customers, suppliers and employees, all offering suggestions as to how to make a good service even better.

These actions developed and reinforced the strategic priorities of efficiency, awareness and customer satisfaction—and they made EasyJet popular, distinctive and successful in a very competitive market. The launch by British Airways of a rival low-fare airline, Go, only flattered EasyJet, who eventually acquired the business.

Innovation can be seen as needless change, or it can be welcomed as an opportunity for people to contribute their ideas and to create value, which benefits the whole organisation. At a personal level, innovation allows individuals to engage energetically with new challenges, with little chance of work becoming stale or lacking stimulation. Also, problems are more easily solved and new opportunities created, while people are better able to learn, gain new perspectives and develop valuable skills.

Challenge 5: focus on customers

Understanding customers, market developments and technology leads to customer-focused decisions and these, in turn, provide the most certain route to profitability. There is a challenge, however, in developing a keen understanding of where a market is heading and how opportunities can be exploited. It is easy to dismiss customer-focused decisions as self-evident, whereas in reality it is often difficult to incorporate customer issues into decisions.

> 'Customer focus' is a frequently repeated phrase. Despite this, the difficulty is to sustain a level of consistent customer focus in such a way that the firm's activities are continually informed and improved.

Customer focus matters because this is how firms retain their existing customers and sell more to them, while also attracting new business from elsewhere. Turn to Chapter 4 for advice on how to sustain customer focus, and to Chapters 5 and 6 for methods of selling and increasing revenue.

Challenge 6: develop business relationships

Relationships are at the heart of how people and organisations work. Our careers, achievements and a large part of our happiness rest on our ability to relate to others successfully. Despite all of this, it's rare that we focus on the skills and attributes needed for strong business relationships. It's certainly an area to work on, however, as failed or failing businesses are characterised by weak relationships. Put another way, strong business relationships—internally, among employees, and externally, with customers, suppliers and others—help a business to succeed.

Ignore relationships at your peril: they generate profits and enable people to achieve their potential. Relationships underpin many of the toughest business challenges:

- *Building trusting relationships with colleagues, helping them to keep and develop their people.* You can also increase the effectiveness of their teams and enhance job satisfaction by, for example, sharing knowledge, innovating and collaborating, delivering value for customers, retaining clients and acquiring new business and by attracting and getting the best from people
- *Developing trusting relationships with external contacts,* notably clients, but also other stakeholders, in a way that develops profitable new business
- *Excelling at the intangibles of business and personal success*—for example, understanding, motivation, trust, assertiveness, loyalty, collaboration, confidence, respect, innovation, diversity, responsibility and flexibility
- *Developing, in practical ways, skills of persuasion, influence and emotional intelligence*
- *Coaching and developing other people* so that their skills come to the fore
- *Leading teams with inspiration, passion and purpose* by enhancing their ability to manage with empathy and integrity

Surviving a downturn relies, to a surprising degree, on the ability to cultivate an atmosphere and expectation of trust. You need to trust others and they need to trust you, and this starts with you taking responsibility for creating the trust.

Julian Richer, founder of the successful UK hi-fi chain Richer Sounds, has developed a rewarding and trust-based business that has a waiting list of people wanting to work there. One of his key principles is that the sales staff take responsibility for doing what they think is appropriate to make the customer happy. To enable them to do that confidently, there is an in-depth training programme that covers product knowledge, building relationships and how to handle a range of challenging situations. The new sales person also has a colleague who takes care of them and mentors them in their first few months. And they are all called 'colleagues' through a sense of respect. So Julian Richer has set up the 'rules of engagement' as well as putting in place training and support systems that provide a framework within which people can be trusted to do what they consider to be right.

In meeting this challenge, it can be said that the better the relationship, the more the business will prosper. Chapter 9 explains how company owners or managers can develop the quality of their relationships, both for short-term results and long-term growth.

Challenge 7: don't spend too much on the wrong things or too little on the right ones

In the words of the celebrated economist J. K. Galbraith, 'There can be few fields of human endeavour in which history counts for so little as in the world of finance.'

Cash is in many ways like water: everyone wants it, it's hard to control and it flows away very easily. Businesses most often get into a downturn because they ignore customers or cash. They then struggle to get out of trouble because they have no money to spend, or—more likely—they spend it on the wrong things.

Also, firms in a downturn tend not to focus on all the right questions. For example, a business owner or manager may ask,

'Where are we wasting money?', which is, of course, a vital question. However, this can overshadow another equally important issue: 'Where can we get the greatest impact from the money we *do* have?' This recognises that some money isn't being wasted on wholly unproductive activities: it just isn't the right moment to spend on this activity in preference to another. One of the secrets of surviving a downturn is therefore not simply to cut expenditure, but to re-evaluate and redirect it. Timing can be at least as important, here, as the amount spent.

Another possibly unhelpful question is, 'How do we find more customers?', when what you really need is to increase your revenue. You can do this by raising prices (if the market will stand it) or by selling more to existing customers. A more appropriate question would be, 'How can we increase the amount of money coming into the business?'

Managing cash effectively, cutting costs and bumping up revenues and external investment will all help. What succeeds is an approach that is rigorous and combines trusty (if dull) conventional methods with a deep understanding of what the business can do to turn the corner. If you focus your financial resources well, success is much more likely. Also, manage the basics, from cash flow to revenue. Turn to Chapters 3 and 7 for more help on this key issue.

The threat of moral hazard

During tough economic times, risks and incentives are fluid. It is vital to understand how this affects individuals within a market. Moral hazard occurs when someone behaves differently because they are shielded from a particular risk—so that some don't face the consequences of their actions as they have passed them onto others. One cause of moral hazard is asymmetry of information, where one party has better product information or a better ability to sense the future of the market than another. A good example of this is a used car salesperson whose cars are faulty. Unless there is sufficient regulation they will be able to profit from selling cars for more than they are worth with the buyers facing the consequences of this and losing out. The consequence of moral hazard is market failure: however, this is so pervasive in certain markets, that the only way to protect oneself is to ensure that one is not acting with inferior information. Only by being both self and market aware, can you ensure you are not making flawed decisions based on corrupt information.

Navigating around black swans

Following Lehman Brothers' bankruptcy in 2008, the threat of what Taleb calls 'Black Swan Events', (Nassim Nicholas Taleb, *The Black Swan*, Penguin, 2007) have been shown to provide a significant disruptive effect during any downturn. These events are 'outliers', with very low expected probabilities, but which present the potential for significant disruption. Taleb illustrates this with the example of the First World War: most statesmen at the beginning of 1914 thought the outbreak of war as so remote as to be fantastical, yet by the end of the year, the Great Powers were embroiled in a conflict in which millions eventually perished and which remade international politics. In the 20th Century, the development of the Internet had a disruptive impact—but it was foreseen by very few. Success is not predicated on accurate prediction of Black Swan events, which is impossible. Rather, success derives from a strategic readiness to maximize opportunities that arise from the unknown and to embrace change.

Are you facing a downturn?
Ask yourself the following:

WHAT CAUSES A BUSINESS DOWNTURN?

1. **Are you generating less profit than before?**
   Specifically, is your profit in the last 12 months lower than the profit of the 12 months before that?
   (An economy is said to be in recession when gross domestic product (GDP) declines for three consecutive quarters. Similarly, you should consider that your firm is in recession if your profit declines for consecutive periods. These could be weeks, months or quarters, depending on the nature of your business.)
   Also, you may be in (or entering) a downturn if:

   - you don't know how much profit you are making
   - profits are declining
   - profits are similar to, or the same as, before in an expanding market

2. **Are people leaving your business faster than this time last year?**
3. **What are your key measures of performance indicating?** For example, what is your ratio of costs to sales, debtor days (that is, how quickly you get paid) or productivity?
4. **What is the trend for the following indicators of business performance? Are they getting better or worse?**

   - sales revenue in the last year
   - sales revenue in the last month
   - number of new customers
   - number of loyal customers
   - number of competitors
   - volume sold

- time taken to sell one unit
- profit per unit
- sales cost per unit
- direct costs
- overheads

These figures are, of course, interrelated. But if even just one of these indicators is worsening, you've got a problem. If two or more show a downward trend, you're probably facing a downturn.

A good friend of mine who is a teacher once said that 'revision starts when the course starts'. In the same way, it's never too soon to start surviving a downturn by increasing awareness of potential problems and being on the alert for warning signs.

2 PRACTICAL TECHNIQUES FOR BOOSTING PROFITABILITY

Boosting profitability is the biggest challenge for businesses of all sizes and the one that comes under most pressure during a downturn—so much so that other commercial objectives such as growing the business or being socially responsible can fall out of focus.

It's crucial to understand what profitability is, how it is achieved and increased. Above all, you need to understand the practical techniques for boosting profitability during those tough times when profits are most at risk.

Boosting a business's profitability is a simple concept to grasp: it means increasing revenues and reducing costs. The challenge is to make it happen. Read on to find out how.

Develop the right strategy

By being better at what you do, you can boost profitability. You may also become more profitable by *changing* what you currently do. However, while going down that route may generate greater rewards, it also carries a greater degree of risk.

> Having an effective strategy will differentiate business and provide the impetus for success. A weak or misunderstood strategy can be equally significant and can drive a company out of business.

A corporate strategy has three essential elements: development, implementation and selling. Underpinning all three is choice; in particular, the need for you as the business owner to choose a distinctive strategic position on three considerations:

1. **who to target as customers (and who to avoid targeting)**
2. **what products to offer**
3. **how to undertake related activities**

In every industry there are several viable positions that a company can occupy. The essence of strategy therefore is to choose the *one* position that your company will claim as its own. A strategic position is simply the sum of a company's answers to the three questions above. The goal for every company should be to answer these questions differently from its competitors. If you can do that, your business can stake out a unique strategic position.

The need to make clear, successful choices when developing strategy is best shown by the example of Nespresso™, one of the most innovative products developed by Swiss giant Nestlé. The product is a system that allows consumers to produce a fresh cup of espresso coffee at home. Though simple in appearance and easy to use, Nestlé spent more than ten years developing the product.

Nespresso was introduced in 1986 as a joint venture between Nespresso and a Swiss-based distributor called Sobal. The new venture, Sobal-Nespresso, purchased the coffee-making machines from another Swiss company, Turmix, and the coffee capsules from Nestlé. Sobal-Nespresso would then distribute and sell everything as a system: one product, one price. Offices and restaurants were targeted as customers and a separate unit called Nespresso S. A. was set up within Nestlé to support the joint venture's sales and marketing efforts and to service and maintain the machines.

By 1988, the business had failed to take off and those at headquarters were considering freezing the operation. This was definitely a business in a downturn. However, in 1988–89 Jean-Paul Gaillard, commercial director of Nespresso, introduced a new strategy. This turned the operation round and established the unit as a profitable and growing enterprise within Nestlé. Gaillard introduced several changes, but underpinning all his actions was the belief that the coffee side of the operation had to be separated from the machine side. Since Nestlé was not in the machine business, he felt he had to focus on the coffee.

The manufacture of the Nespresso machine was assigned to a Swiss-based manufacturer, which then supplied several carefully selected manufacturers, such as Krups, Turmix and Philips. These companies, in turn, sold the Nespresso machine to prestigious retailers that included Harrods, Galeries Lafayette and Bloomingdale's. It was the responsibility of the retailers, under the guidance and control of Nespresso, to promote, demonstrate and finally sell the machine to the end-consumer. It was also the responsibility of the machine partners (Krups and Philips, for example) to service and maintain the machines.

On the coffee side, the Sobal partnership was terminated and the whole operation placed under Nespresso S. A. (later Nestlé Coffee

Specialties S. A.). The target customer was changed from offices to households, and the distribution of coffee capsules was organised through a 'club'. Once customers bought a machine they became a member of the Nespresso Club. Orders for capsules were made over the phone or by fax direct to the club, and the capsules were shipped to the customer's home within 24 hours. The club currently takes 7,000 orders per day.

Nespresso made clear and explicit choices concerning whom to target, what to sell and how to do this. The original choices did not produce the desired results. The choices made by Jean-Paul Gaillard in 1988–89, however, have rejuvenated Nespresso and turned it into a profitable unit of Nestlé.

NESTLÉ'S STRATEGIC CHOICES

Who	Who should I target as customers?	Target individuals and households, *not* restaurants or offices.
What	What products or services should I offer?	• Sell coffee, not coffee machines.
		• Educate retailers so that they can teach the end-consumer how to use the machine.
How	How can I best deliver the product to customers?	• Subcontract the manufacture of the Nespresso machine to a prestigious manufacturer.
		• Focus on the production of high-quality coffee capsules.
		• Sell the Nespresso machine through prestigious retailers.
		• Sell the coffee capsules direct through the Nespresso Club.

The strategy can also be applied if you're attempting to complete a smaller task or role. This may appear to be less grand but it's often just as important: frequently, progress towards achieving the overall business strategy happens when you find ways to achieve the supporting tasks.

Enabling people to respond to a downturn in a way that is focused on boosting profitability is a major leadership challenge. Thereafter, several challenges need to be mastered in order to boost profits, including:

- **focusing on developing current (or most promising) areas of profitability**
- **increasing audacity and entrepreneurship**
- **choosing the right path to growth**

Challenge 1: Focus on areas of profitability

As most businesses operate in more than one market, they have to decide how to carve up costs between those markets and all related activities. As you'd imagine, the best thing to do is to concentrate resources on the most profitable areas; if one business line is making a loss, it would make sense to pull out of that market. Similarly, if you suspect that it'd be profitable to enter a new market, you'll need to channel resources there instead. The strategy of building a profitable company is about choosing those business activities that will bring in the most revenue.

For example, when Jack Welch was CEO of the giant US corporation General Electric, he held the policy that GE would have either the greatest, or the second greatest, share in each market in which it was engaged. If GE were, say, fifth in the market (or worse), they'd pull out. In parallel with this, Welch ensured the business stayed in touch with global economic trends and took new opportunities to enter potentially profitable markets. This tactic help him to refocus GE. He reduced expenditure on unprofitable activities while increasing investment in the most lucrative areas and developing new profitable products.

While your business won't be on the GE scale, there are plenty of useful lessons to be drawn from Jack Welch's tactics.

Develop profitable new products

Too often during a downturn, managers assume that falling demand and rising competition will make product development risky and unprofitable. This is understandable, perhaps, but it ignores two important facts:

1. While it may be risky to develop a new product in a changing market, doing *nothing* is even riskier: the momentum of innovation will carry your business beyond the downturn. If you stay the same during a period of increased competition and falling demand, you'll end up falling even further and faster behind your competitors.
2. If the general market is in a downturn because demand has fallen, it doesn't mean that every single lucrative commercial opportunity has vanished. For instance, during a downturn people often change their buying habits. If you can understand how they do this before your competitors do, you can change the way you do business to capture market share. Don't simply accept failure: go out and look for opportunities in unlikely places. What have you got to lose?

Managing product development can also boost profitability. Think about:

- **the amount spent on developing a product.** Different methods will have different effects on profitability: more expensive techniques will reduce profitability, unless they become a unique selling point of the product. If this is the case, your sales revenue will get a boost.
- **shelf-life and duration of the product's appeal.** When will the product need to be replaced? Realistically, how long will people continue to buy the product? For instance, computers and clothes tend to stay on the market for a short period of time, while chocolate bars can be marketed for much longer. This affects the product's profitability, as it affects the volume of sales and the need to invest in replacing the product.
- **target market, segments and customer appeal of the product.** To maximise a new product's profitability, match customers with sales techniques and make sure that it's sold 'appropriately'—in a way that will best engage with, and appeal to, the target market. Be sure that you understand who the product is aimed at before you launch headlong into marketing it.
- **number and quality of suppliers or business partners.** Decide what the buying policy should be. Would be best to use a small number of preferred suppliers or set up a bidding system among a wider number of potential suppliers? Also think about techniques for controlling delivery charges, monitoring exchange rates, improving quality control, reducing stockholding and improving production lead times.

New product development often focuses on market need or production issues, without paying enough attention to customers, cost, price and sales volume, all of which are inextricably linked to profitability. (For certain products in certain markets, lower prices may actually *reduce* demand.)

> Given the barriers to entry and exit, ask 'Is it worth being engaged in this market? Are there other, more promising opportunities?'

To focus your business activities, make sure you understand:

- **the profitability of existing business lines**
- **the potential for new opportunities**
- **the market exit and entry barriers for each**

The ease and difficulty of both entering and exiting a market are crucial factors in managing profitability. Entry barriers include the need to compete with businesses that are enjoying economies of scale, or who are challenging established, differentiated products. Other barriers include capital (ie, cash) requirements, access to distribution channels, factors independent of scale (such as technology or location) and regulatory barriers imposed by government or industry associations. When markets are difficult or expensive to enter and relatively easy and affordable to leave, firms can achieve high, stable returns, while still being able to leave for other opportunities. Where do the barriers to entry lie for your market? How vulnerable you are to new entrants? Is it possible for you to strengthen your position in the market?

Decide how to manage the least profitable products

The least profitable products often drift, which means that profitability dwindles. If this is happening to you, take decisive action to turn round a poor performer: you could, for example, cut costs, increase prices, alter discounts, change the product or abandon it altogether to prevent a drain on resources and reputation. Don't be afraid of taking this latter option: if it's genuinely the best option, do it. See Challenge 4 below.

Focus decisions on the most profitable areas

Concentrating on products and services with the best margin will protect or enhance profitability. This might involve redirecting sales and advertising activities, but it will be worth it. There are plenty of other ways that you can use those resources, so don't waste time and money on anything that isn't profitable unless it can be turned round and made successful.

Use ratio analysis

This supports business decisions and helps to boost profitability. A ratio is simply a relationship between two numbers, but, when compared to like ratios for previous periods, they can show important trends and patterns in performance. To avoid problems when using ratios, ask the following questions.

- **Which ratio is most appropriate?**
- **What is the trend: how is the ratio developing and why?**
- **How reliable is the data on which the ratio is based?**
- **What comparisons are desirable in using a ratio?**

By comparing to key performance indicators for your business, you can better understand performance. The process highlights areas that aren't as profitable as they should be, prompting you to act to boost profitability or to get out of the market.

- **Gross profit** highlights the relationship between *revenue* and *costs of sale*. If gross profit is too low, it could either mean that prices are too low or costs are too high.
- **Net profit** examines the relationship between *revenue* and *total costs*. If it is too low or falling, then costs may be rising or revenue falling. With both profit ratios it is important to closely monitor *trends* (that it, whether profits are falling, static or rising) as well as identifying what part of the business is causing the problem, and then taking immediate action.
- **Sales growth** is measured by dividing sales for the period by sales for a previous period. The period that is chosen can be highly significant: the shorter it is (a day or a week), the more sensitive the ratio becomes. Shorter periods are more relevant for reflecting seasonal demand.
- **Value of work in hand** indicates the size of a firm's order book. It is calculated by dividing the value of orders in hand by the average value of daily sales. Analysis of this ratio over an extended period reveals trends in sales performance. Large fluctuations may indicate instability or vulnerability.
- **Marketing efficiency (sales to cost ratio)** is calculated as a percentage of revenue and is marketing spend divided by revenue. When budgeting, for example, it is useful to know how much money needs to be devoted to marketing to generate a given level of sales.
- **Market share** should be read alongside the sales growth ratio. This is calculated by dividing current market share by

previous market share. If market share is being taken together with sales growth, the periods need to be similar. Ratios of the market share of each product can be compared between periods to see which markets and product groups are most profitable. This highlights strengths and weaknesses in a product portfolio and can be used to gauge a product's position in its life cycle. If it is declining, decide if it is a long-term trend, or a short-term blip in need of corrective action.

- **Average debtor collection period,** showing how long debtors take to pay, helps to manage cash flow and ensure that collection periods are as short as possible, which, because money is worth more now than money in the future, reduces costs.

- **Average creditor payment period** shows how long the business takes to pay its debts, and can be calculated in a similar way, substituting creditors for debtors and cost of sales for actual sales.

- **Stock (inventory) turnover** is often used in manufacturing and retailing businesses to indicate the presence of slow moving stock or too much stock, which impedes cash flow.

- **The current ratio** is the ratio of current (also known as present) assets to liabilities. It should normally be between 1.5 and 2; if it is less than 1, current liabilities exceed current assets and the business could be insolvent. For some industries it should be over 2 on the grounds that half the assets might be stock.

- **The quick or acid test ratio** is a more rigorous test of liquidity. It takes into account the fact that some current assets, such as stock or work in progress, may be difficult to turn into cash quickly. Deducting these from the current assets gives the quick assets. The quick ratio is normally between 0.7 and 1; if the quick ratio is 1 or more, then quick assets exceed current liabilities and the business is safe. (Note: if the current ratio is rising and the quick ratio is largely unchanged, this implies there is a stockholding problem.)

■ **Price/earnings (P/E) ratio** is the share price divided by the earnings per share (EPS). This ratio is the one that investors and analysts focus on, and it forms part of the valuation of a company during acquisitions and disposals. The higher the ratio, the more the company is deemed to be worth, although there are several points to note. P/E ratios vary across industry sectors and in different countries, and they are relative to those of competitors. They rise when the share price rises, for example, or when there is speculation about a merger or takeover. Also, they can lag behind events, combining current share price with past earnings. A P/E ratio may, for instance, be too high compared to likely future growth.

Challenge 2: Rediscover your inner entrepreneur

Beyond focusing your business on what it does well and doing less of what it does badly, boosting profitability involves capitalising on opportunities. By being audacious and entrepreneurial, you can find potentially profitable opportunities. In practice, this means finding better ways to understand markets and customers.

Boosting profitability is not merely about understanding your business and applying best practices to control costs, increase sales, enter and leave markets. It is about being creative, innovative, flexible and, above all, audacious. This can be difficult, however, involving as it does charting a course between being too conservative—an unwillingness to embrace change and risk—and throwing caution to the wind.

Boosting profitability by being audacious involves three elements:

1. **increasing awareness**
2. **building self-confidence and taking control**
3. **establishing a compelling vision**

Increasing awareness

This means understanding both what you do and what your situation is. Keeping in touch with both during a downturn is critical as it's all too easy to get 'out of touch' with the market. Reflect on and question what is going on, so that you understand what you *are* doing and what you *should* be doing to boost profitability, a necessary first step towards closing the gap.

Building self-confidence and taking control

Many opportunities possess a dangerous edge, an inherent risk, which must be managed, but it is also important to be confident in your ability to overcome potential pitfalls to boost profitability. The risk implies a greater return on your investment. While it is worth being concerned about the risk, consider how you can take control of the situation to minimise the dangers. Rather than just accepting threats to your business, take control and influence customers in order to minimise the threat of falling demand.

Establishing a compelling vision

A vision is what motivates you to take risks. People will not be brought along and motivated if they are not given a compelling vision. Moreover, it is better to brainstorm practical techniques when you understand what it is you are trying to achieve. Techniques for boosting profitability are a series of choices, rather than a mathematical formula for success, where if you apply them in the right proportions they equal profit. What would suit your business best? What are your values? Are you risk-averse? Do you manage costs ruthlessly to offer value to customers, or do you spend more time and money finding the best suppliers to improve quality and increase sales revenue?

> The techniques you use to boost profitability must be consistent with your organisation's vision.

Challenge 3: Choose the right path to growth

One of the most fundamental decisions for any business is choosing the most effective strategy for growth. The five ways of profitably growing a business are:

1. **organic growth**
2. **mergers and acquisitions**
3. **integration**
4. **diversification**
5. **specialisation**

All these are limited by the resources available—during a downturn, for instance, cash tends to be scarcer—and require a clear focus on objectives and a sustained level of commitment. When you're making decisions affecting business growth, keep in mind the basic economic principle that value is always associated with scarcity. Providing something that people can get hold of easily from other sources isn't likely to result in much profit. If you want your company to get the most from its customers, attract new business and increase revenues and profits, explore the issue of scarcity, now and in the future.

Organic growth

This type of growth occurs when a business grows from its own resources. Typically, it arises because of a growing existing market, but it can also result from the development of new markets or from more effective marketing and sales operations. Organic growth is difficult during a downturn, largely because of falling demand. Exploiting a product advantage—a law firm with a star partner, say, or a software firm with a unique program—can sustain it to a certain extent, but it becomes vulnerable. For example, if the partner retires or the software become obsolete, you're on dangerous ground. Also, the capacity to grow is finite, and will eventually reach a plateau.

Mergers and acquisitions

One of the highest profile strategic options to boost profitability by growing your business is the acquisition or merger. These are notoriously difficult, fraught with risk and complexity and with many issues threatening failure or disaster. With the media loudly highlighting any disasters associated with mergers and acquisitions, such as that of RBS and ABN Amro, Daimler-Benz and Chrysler,

Compaq and Hewlett-Packard, AOL and Time Warner, the pitfalls of mergers and acquisitions are far more widely known than the advantages. Mergers and acquisitions (M&A) are increasingly important for many firms, especially medium and large undertakings and those operating in more than one market.

At the time of writing, M&A activity is relatively quiet, with firms reacting to current economic uncertainties and stock market fluctuations with a cautious conservatism. It won't last: M&A is such a potentially powerful route to growth and competitive advantage that as soon as economic confidence returns, so will M&A mania. Even before then, plucky entrepreneurs and bold shareholders may see opportunities to pick up a bargain, such as a sound business that may have encountered short-term difficulties. Surviving a downturn is about capitalising on such opportunities. However, problems are common following business mergers. An enquiry published in the *Harvard Business Review* (November 1997) demonstrated that:

> 'Fewer than 50% of mergers ever reach anywhere near the economic or strategic destination that was envisioned for them. In fact, in many cases the mergers fail because the new company's managers underestimated, ignored, or mishandled the integration tasks.'

Ensuring that a merger or acquisition succeeds is difficult, complex and full of problems. Success hinges on mastering the skills of the three main stages of the merger or acquisition process, and the decisions associated with each.

1. **Planning and preparation: the first step is to develop an effective strategy, including a 'top-down' vision**

based on the advantages of acquisition versus other approaches, such as joint ventures or organic growth. This vision determines how the business approaches the deal, what is to be gained, likely targets or partners and the rationale for the deal. Coupled with this is the 'bottom-up' approach, where senior managers at subsidiary level understand and influence strategy. They can pinpoint potential pitfalls as well as more positive future developments that may be overlooked, as well as providing a source of information. This can range from advising on a target's actual strengths and weaknesses to identifying specific opportunities quickly and routinely. Before beginning a merger or acquisition, you need to consider certain issues, including the:

- deal's objectives
- current and potential value of the target business
- organisational culture of the two businesses
- price of the target
- attitude of stakeholders (notably shareholders and key customers in both businesses)

2. Due diligence is the process of investigating the target company in detail. The benefit of due diligence is not only in producing a financial and legal audit that helps you to understand the target company's value, but also understanding the culture of the business and the nature of its activities to ensure the acquisition is successful. Due diligence involves examining the target's accounts, contracts and all

aspects of the commercial situation. It provides a basis for identifying and avoiding risks, ensuring accurate valuation and preparing for post-acquisition integration.

3. Post-acquisition integration: an effective post-acquisition strategy is a vital component of successful acquisitions. It maximises the profitability of the resulting company after the deal is done. Post-acquisition integration should take into account:

- strategic issues affecting the new business
- the culture and management styles of the two organisations; the strengths of both should be merged to eliminate weaknesses
- issues of presentation, communication and understanding
- customer focus: How will customers, current and potential, react to the merger? How can this be turned to the firm's advantage?
- people issues: How will employees react to the merger? How will it affect their motivation, empowerment and innovation?

Integration

This boosts profitability and involves working closer with other businesses in the same industry. Obviously, mergers and acquisitions are one way of doing this, but integration is a broader strategy. It can refer to partnership deals, joint ventures and other strategic alliances.

Integration can be 'vertical' or 'horizontal'. Vertical integration involves business in the same industry but at different stages of the value chain (for example, PepsiCo acquiring restaurants to sell its drinks). Vertical integration can provide businesses with greater control over the process of getting their products to the end user because it can provide access to a range of resources, from customers to sources of supply, distribution or essential processes.

In contrast, horizontal integration involves the collaboration of organisations in the same industry. An example of this is in the printing industry, where, perhaps to win a specific contract, a printer specialising in book production may link with a printer specialising in multimedia production in order to offer their customers a complete and integrated service. Horizontal integration can provide economies of scale, as well as enhancing the size, expertise and credibility of both businesses. During a downturn, with increased competitive pressures, rising costs and slumping demand, integration (and the extra market power it provides) helps to maintain competitiveness.

Diversification

Diversification involves a business moving into another area of activity. This takes advantage of a potentially profitable market and can reduce the risk faced by a business, as changes in one market affect a smaller proportion of gross profit.

A core technique for boosting profitability during a downturn: be innovative in the way you use what you have, so that you can do more with it. Are you getting maximum value from every resource?

Diversification can either mean launching a new product in an existing market (for example, an established national airline starting a low-cost service) or a new product in a different market (for example, an established airline buying a rail franchise and operating train services). Developing partnerships and integrating your business can help to achieve diversification, which also provides synergies between activities in the two markets.

Diversification is challenging but it can provide major new opportunities for existing skills and spare capacity. For example, an advertising agency may transform itself into a video production company producing corporate videos, because it possesses the necessary skills and resources. This is known as concentric diversification, where existing skills, customers and sales channels are at the core, but the applications broaden in concentric rings. This highlights a core technique for boosting profitability to survive a downturn: innovatively use what you have to do more.

Specialisation

The opposite of diversification, specialisation involves dropping non-essential activities, or even redefining core operations and focusing on them. If it is not profitable to stay in a market, and if making activities in that market sufficiently profitable would be too difficult, get out of it. If your business focuses on the core markets in which it performs best, it can survive a downturn by boosting profitability. Engaging in underperforming markets, on the other hand, may cost you valuable cash.

The main advantage of specialisation is a clear focus, as all available resources are channelled into either one endeavour or a select few. Cash available from the sale of non-core operations can be used to grow the business.

However, the profitability of specialisation depends on the barriers to exit of the market you are trying to leave: mobile phone companies that have bought a five-year licence to operate a service in a particular country may find that the amount they have already spent to get into the market—which they cannot get back simply by exiting—makes it prudent to stay put. Moreover, it is vital to remember that you cannot contract your way to growth.

Challenge 4: Boost product profitability

Your next challenge is to make your priority activities as profitable as possible. In 1992, IBM made one of the largest losses in US corporate history and subsequently changed the nature of their business altogether, leaving entire markets and entering others.

We have explored the techniques that a company in such a position can use to change and refocus their business to be more profitable. It is also important to understand, given the prevailing market conditions, how the profitability of operations can be increased. This is about best practice: learning and developing the skills needed to increase sales revenue and reduce costs. Building a profitable business with a blend of popular, valued products requires innovation and creativity. You'll also need consistency and tenacity; rather than abandoning a particular market for a product, you'll have to make that market work. To do so requires constant effort to find effective new strategies and tactics, applying special attention to detail, and it is vital to surviving a downturn.

Techniques for boosting the profitability of an individual product depend on the factors that affect its profitability. One way of thinking about this is to consider what is wrong with the product's profitability, and then do something about it. If costs are too high, sales are weakened by deteriorating quality or functionality, or sales channels are ineffective, fix it. Another way to think about this—also appropriate for launching a new product—is to look at all the factors affecting profitability and make sure you're actively managing each one. By so doing you will have boosted the profitability of the product in every way possible.

Increase sales revenue

Boosting revenue will, of course, boost profitability. It can be most often achieved by:

- **increasing the effectiveness of your sales teams, sales process, sales activities and channels—or a combination of all four. An invaluable technique here is *measurement*: what gets measured gets done; measurement influences behaviour and helps continuous learning and improvement. For example, if you measure the time it takes each sales person to convert a sale, from start to finish, then this highlights to them that you consider sales lead times a priority, and it does so in a constructive way that might actually help them understand the issues and improve their performance.**
- **broadening and deepening the appeal of your product to customers. It's often thought that the problem lies with sales and marketing activities when the solution is much simpler: what is really needed is a better product. This may mean a major new process of product development; on the other hand, you may just need a better understanding of your customers and what they value, coupled with**

the imagination to tweak an existing product to give it an edge.

Xerox can illustrate this for us again. Having recovered from its difficulties in the 1970s, Xerox found itself in dire straits once more in 2000. Anne Mulcahy, then the new CEO, took time to speak to customers and front-line employees and found that Xerox products were simply outmoded. One of the firm's top priorities was to focus resources on creating new products. By 2005, two thirds of its revenues came from products launched within the preceding two years, a move that undoubtedly helped to save the company from catastrophe.

Also, improving the effectiveness of your sales strategy will boost profitability, both because it increases revenue and because a more effective strategy reduces the cost of making a sale. Sales proposals occur more frequently than you might think. While a face-to-face sales meeting with a client is what is traditionally thought of as a 'sales proposal', it can actually be any opportunity you have to sell—such as writing a sales e-mail or picking up the phone to a prospective client—and so refers to the process that moves a potential sales lead to make a purchase. Don't take too narrow a view of what constitutes a sales proposal, as you may be ignoring opportunities.

In his seminal book *How to Win Friends and Influence People*, Dale Carnegie stresses the importance of how you *deliver* a sales proposal and how it is *perceived*. Sales means meeting customers' needs; work out what people want and then show how your product meets that demand. Also remember that, rather than telling your client something, a successful proposal *sells* them something. Highlight the benefits to customers in a way that will appeal most to them—don't simply explain the product's features. Also try to master the **seven stages of making a sale** (see pp. 97–98):

1. **getting yourself accepted: building credibility and rapport**
2. **stating your intent**
3. **asking the right questions that underline your USPs (unique selling points)**
4. **checking you are addressing the buyer's problems appropriately**
5. **providing solutions to the buyer's problems**
6. **checking the buyer is happy (this may mean the end user as well as the purchaser)**
7. **closing the deal**

Innovate with price

Price innovations can be achieved by changing any of the factors relating to the product. For example, a food manufacturer may wish to launch a new size of product with a new price; a lawyer or accountant may stop charging a per diem rate and instead offer a flat rate for clients. A higher price for a large piece of equipment or machinery may be offset by extended payment terms. Many issues affect price: customers may value and pay more for a pricing system which better fits their needs. By being creative about how you charge for a product, you can influence the price elasticity of demand of your product (p.e.d. = the ratio of a change in demand to a change in price). The vital issue of pricing is explored further in Chapter 5.

Challenge 5: Control costs

Boosting profitability is achieved by reducing and/or delaying costs, which we explore in detail in Chapter 6. Also important are:

1. **reducing risks.** Understanding where risks lie and what needs to happen to reduce risk is an important part of financial decision-making. For example, you need to know not only where the break-even point is for a product, but also how and when it will be reached.

2. **balancing costs and quality.** You need to get the best value possible from your suppliers and will need to strike a balance between price paid and quality received. Can your suppliers provide you with significantly greater value at little or no additional cost?

3. **remembering that financial decisions affect everyone.** Finance has an impact on every aspect of the organisation. Don't leave financial decisions entirely to the 'experts' in the finance department or to specialist advisers: every single person in the business with a financial responsibility should be kept in the loop.

4. **managing production and suppliers.** Production costs can be one of the biggest costs for a business, so monitor them closely and control them to ensure profitability. They also contain hidden risks that are often overlooked. During a downturn, what would you do if a major supplier went bankrupt, or drastically increased its prices? Production does not just affect costs; it also affects sales. Customers value and pay attention to production: for example, 'fair-trade' coffees, which are produced ethically, are increasingly popular, and customers have boycotted companies with noticeably unethical production policies. Production costs also relate closely to issues of quality and delivery time, which have a significant impact on profitability.

5. **monitoring and influencing sales and customer issues.** Markets exert the greatest influence on profits; without

revenue, there is no profit. Some of the most important factors to measure and manage include:

- **sales expenses (such as travel costs per sales person)**
- **the number of leads generated, customers served and revenue or profit generated per sales employee**
- **marketing and advertising response rates and marketing effectiveness**
- **image, reputation and quality of the business**
- **levels of customer satisfaction**
- **levels of repeat business from existing customers**
- **pricing and discounts—are these competitive, attractive and viable?**

Challenge 6: Manage your cash

Cash is the lifeblood of any business and it needs to be managed carefully during a downturn. Your cash-flow forecasts will affect the decisions you take, so they need to be as accurate and realistic as possible.

Cash management also affects profitability. If your business doesn't have enough cash and needs to borrow some, you'll incur costs in the form of interest. The 'time value' of money (ie, the fact that the value of money reduces over time) is a factor that can reduce profitability, and this is particularly relevant when you're thinking about investment decisions and trying to gauge their potential profitability. Other relevant and related issues include:

- **the time customers take to pay debts (also, the level of debtors and the average age of accounts outstanding)**

- credit control policies and procedures
- the number of bad debts (especially their frequency and severity)

Challenge 7: Seek and seize commercial opportunities

It's important to be bold and creative when you aim to boost the profitability of an existing product, just as you'd need to be if you were planning to enter a new market or launch a new product. For instance, could an existing product be sold to new customers? One way of seizing commercial opportunities is to add 'profit-boosting initiatives' to regular meeting agendas, and to discuss (or brainstorm) commercial ideas. This encourages other people in your business to be creative about how you engage with a market. Form a team with colleagues to identify and try out initiatives, as well as learning from other initiatives around the business. Find ways to share expertise and experience, and encourage your team to develop ideas.

Challenge 8: Develop people's skills

Active, successful leadership is essential for profitability. People need to feel supported and when you're the boss, you need to lead the charge. Keep everyone in the loop by communicating clearly, helping out as much as you can and by rewarding people fairly for their work. Money will be tight during a downturn, but provide training and development opportunities where you can. By giving people the skills to produce and market a product, and confidence in what they are doing, they'll end up doing it better, which in turn will raise quality, efficiency and profitability. For example, ask yourself: 'Do my people know exactly what is expected of them? Do they have all enough support to achieve their objectives?' If they don't, they're probably confused and less productive than they could be. Making sure that people are adequately rewarded will not only motivate them but will lead to improved performance and profitability.

Key questions: focusing on profitability

A practical, valuable way to focus on profitability is to address the following key questions:

- **What are the most profitable parts of the business?**
- **What is the trend for profitability in the short, medium and long term?**
- **What are the sources of advantage that are sustaining your profitability (and have sustained it in the past)? How can these be developed?**
- **What are the prospects in the short, medium and long term for other potentially profitable parts?**
- **How precarious is the business? Where is it vulnerable: for example, does it rely on too few products, customers, suppliers, personnel or distribution channels?**
- **How clearly focused is the business? Is it over-burdened with too many products, markets and initiatives, or is it running on empty with too few opportunities on which to capitalise?**
- **What is likely to be the best means of growth?**
- **What are you doing to improve the profitability of existing products?**
- **Can you easily develop valuable new products or service options for customers?**

- Is your problem attracting or retaining customers, sales channels, product quality, product pricing, costs, or something else?
- How can you reduce costs without harming your business? (Remember, few firms have managed to cut their way to growth.)
- Are you gaining maximum value from every resource? How could this be improved?
- Do you understand how the downturn has affected people, their motivation and attitude towards change? What is being done to provide a guiding vision and practical leadership?
- If your business is engaging in a merger or acquisition, how does the merger or acquisition fit with your strategy? What are the main issues faced in making the deal a success? How well is the deal structured? How has post-deal integration been planned? How might issues of organisational culture affect the deal?

3 FOCUSING ON CUSTOMERS

A customer-focused organisation is one that is close to each customer, understanding specific customer types or groups and then using this knowledge when making decisions. Being customer-focused means gathering facts, data and knowledge about both current and potential customers so that you're aware of what they want and how they perceive your products and services. This awareness, together with a keen understanding of where a market is heading and how opportunities can be exploited, will help you to work towards meeting those requirements and in so doing secure your business's long-term survival, growth and profitability. Often, businesses experiencing a downturn have lost touch with their customers, so act quickly to get your focus back.

Why customer focus matters

Customer-focused businesses are good at instilling a passion for excellent customer service across the organisation. These firms make sure that their employees continuously understand, and adapt to, changing customer needs. Customer focus directly increases long-term profitability and competitiveness in three ways:

1. it wins potential customers

2. it captures customers from rivals while keeping your own customers from switching
3. it fights for the best possible share of business from customers who are not exclusively with you or anyone else.

> Understanding customers, market developments and competitors leads to customer-focused decisions, and these provide the most certain route to profitability.

Action checklist: leading a customer-focused business

Use market research objectively
If you have the budget to undertake market research (so that you can understand your customers better), make sure it's well designed, executed and interpreted. It must be objective rather than subjective. Also make sure that it's being done to create insight about the market. The best approach is to use research to refine and update understanding of customer groups.

Stay in touch with customers at a senior level
Make sure that all the decision-makers in your company are in touch with customers, both formally and informally. Customers usually welcome the opportunity to have their voice heard and this simple measure will keep you and your colleagues up to speed with how your products and services are being received.

Involve all employees in thinking about customers

Don't just restrict working on your customer focus to the lucky few: allow everyone to share their knowledge of customers and to use these insights to improve customer service. If your business has a regular meeting for all staff, make sharing thoughts, experiences and ideas on this subject part of your regular agenda.

Make your IT systems work effectively for you

Information systems should be able to give you a clear understanding of customers' preferences and actions. Perhaps surprisingly, many companies' IT systems do not support detailed reporting about customers, to the extent that even some global businesses cannot easily determine who their 20 largest clients are, measured by sales or profitability. Lack of data is a major obstacle to understanding customers and building a clearer understanding of the market. You don't have to spend a fortune, but tackle this issue quickly so that all your hard-won data gives you something back.

Be aware of your competitors

Developing awareness means keeping up to date with the market, knowing how competitors are perceived and why. How do your competitors measure up in terms of:

- **pricing policies and product offers?**
- **brand reputation and customers' perceptions?**
- **product range and quality?**
- **service levels?**
- **organisational factors such as size, economies of scale, type of employees, training, expenditure**

on product development and distribution
channels?
- staff loyalty?
- promotional campaigns: timing, nature and channels
used?

Thanks to the Internet, research of this type needn't be
expensive or time-consuming. Many larger companies now
post their annual report online, and these can be a mine of
information.

Build and exploit sources of competitive advantage

Staying ahead of the competition means acquiring and developing
resources—tangible and intangible—that will make the business
competitive. For example:

- **cash reserves** used to finance sustained marketing
campaigns, innovative development programmes or price
reductions
- **purchasing power and the ability to secure reliable
supply at relatively low costs.** Costs, quality, prices and
delivery can be improved by building close working relations
with preferred suppliers.
- **people are invariably the decisive factor in achieving
success.** A business is only ever as good as the people
working for it. If there is typically a high degree of staff
turnover in the industry, your business might gain an
advantage by recruiting and retaining the best employees. If
flexibility and speed of response is valuable (and it usually is),
get rid of any factors that may interfere with providing
customers with a quick and efficient service. Grumpy

receptionist? Poor packers? Explain that unless they raise their game, you'll have to let them go. Effective leadership is essential here; not having it is actually a competitive *disadvantage*, so gather your courage together and act strongly for the sake of the business.

■ **product factors,** including pricing and discounts, distribution channels, marketing methods, brand reputation and appeal, product quality and how the product relates to others.

Use expertise from other businesses to benefit customers

Do you know of any other businesses that have undertaken successful customer initiatives? If so:

■ **what did they do?**
■ **how did they do it?**
■ **what resources did they need (how expensive were they)?**
■ **what potential pitfalls spring to mind?**
■ **what are the results and benefits?**

Actively encourage others to value customers

As the owner or manager of a business, you have a big role to play when it comes to influencing how your staff interact with customers. For example:

■ **set an example.** When you show that you value each external and internal customer, you set a powerful example that encourages others to do the same. (This works both ways!)

- **give positive feedback.** When you see someone showing that they value a customer, praise that person and let them know that you think it's important. We all tend to repeat behaviour that is recognised and acknowledged.
- **follow up difficult situations.** When you encounter a difficult situation or see someone else trying to deal with one, take a couple of minutes to talk about it afterwards. Focus on learning by asking yourself about what worked and what should be done differently next time.

Over the next week, look for opportunities to encourage others. At the end of each day, make a list of the techniques that you used and what works best for you.

Seek customer feedback

Ask customers for their views on your products and services, both informally as well as formally. You could use tools such as surveys, interviews and focus groups to collect feedback, if budgets allow. Once you have collected the feedback, don't leave it to moulder: develop an action plan to address the issues raised. Most importantly, tell your customers what you are doing to address the issues. For example:

- **ask customers what *one* thing they want above all else. Get them to wave a magic wand and paint their ideal picture. These feelings are often very different from what you might find using hard data alone.**
- **assess the extent to which different customers have different needs. Can you differentiate your market and deliver different services?**

59

- find out what improvements customers want in existing products. How will your customers' needs change in the future?

If you don't usually work directly with customers yourself, spend some time on the front line: dealing with them directly will help you to understand what drives customer value.

Identify your most profitable customers

Customer profitability can be measured by analysing two vital issues: customer revenue and customer costs, including defection and retention costs. (See the table on p. 61.)

- Understanding the issues affecting customer revenue will enable you to understand the customer's reasons for purchasing and what product/ service he/ she values most.
- Assessing the factors affecting cost and how these can be managed, monitored and controlled will improve revenue per customer and focus your sales strategy.
- Identifying the profitability of different customers is an operation closely related to customer relationship management and marketing functions, and it reduces the costs of doing business with the least profitable customers.

Avoiding problems

Adopting a customer-focused approach sounds appealing, ideal and obvious. But what are the potential, practical difficulties? Some examples are given on the following pages pp. 61–3.

ISSUES AFFECTING CUSTOMER REVENUE	ISSUES AFFECTING CUSTOMER COSTS
Revenue per customer	Cost per customer (cost of sale as well as total cost per customer)
Number of orders per customer	Cost per order
Referrals from customers	Cost of retaining customers (cost of loyalty programmes and special offers)
Reasons for not purchasing (or going to a competitor)	Cost of acquiring a new customer
Future needs and likely volume and value of purchases	Likely (or target) growth and future cost implications
Note: understand the reasons for purchasing, what product attributes the customer values most.	Note: assess the factors affecting cost and how these can be managed, monitored and controlled.

THE CHALLENGE . . . AND THE ACTION REQUIRED	
Understanding customers' priorities and market realities	• Research customers' views; request information; and provide incentives for the customer to help to shape your product.
	• Research competitors in the same industry and in other industries, understanding different business models and critical success factors.
	• Meet customers and get them to understand your business. It is never too early to start building trust and loyalty.

THE CHALLENGE . . . AND THE ACTION REQUIRED

Finding ways to improve and innovate	You can improve your customer focus by: • putting yourself in the customer's position • looking at other businesses and industries facing similar issues • brainstorming new approaches, involving everyone in the business When innovating, few things are as frustrating as a raft of initiatives that lack priorities, resources or leadership. A new approach may be needed that • establishes a clear process for new developments • gives innovation a profile among top-level leaders • facilitates knowledge sharing • ensures that best practice expertise is shared • invites and then acts on customer comments.
Hiring and retaining customer-focused people	• Adopt a flexible, imaginative approach staff. A premium is often placed on people with experience of doing things a particular way, when what often matters more is a 'can-do' approach, combining an understanding of what is possible with what is important. • Give people an incentive to generate ideas and implement them.

THE CHALLENGE ... AND THE ACTION REQUIRED

Streamlining business processes	Reviewing existing processes from the customer's viewpoint can help to deliver greater profitability. Understanding what works best and what customers want will count for nothing if it is not effectively implemented.

Dos and don'ts: customer focus

Do

- be clear about what you're offering customers (often called the 'value proposition')
- provide incentives for new customers to return and reorder
- reward established customers' loyalty
- be competitive; what seems like a good deal to you may not be enough to match your competitors in the eyes of your customers
- make the customer's experience as easy and enjoyable as possible
- reassure customers, with a reliable product offer that delivers peace of mind
- continuously improve business processes based on customer feedback

Don't

- over-complicate the product offer; when you're selling something, clarity works
- change the offer too frequently
- ... or stay the same for too long

- avoid asking customers what they think—try to see the purchase from their perspective
- ignore problems and potential pitfalls: identify them early and resolve them or put contingency plans in place should they be needed
- focus on internal divisions; instead, emphasise issues that customers will find most interesting and relevant
- target everyone; focus instead on how to appeal to your most profitable customer groups
- fail to communicate, both internally and externally
- control customers; instead, allow them to feel in control

Key questions: focusing on customers

Understanding your customers

To understand your customers (internal and external), make sure you have open communication channels. Ask yourself:

- How often do I communicate with my customers? Is it enough?
- Do I know my customers' business?
- What do my customers want to achieve? Have I asked them? What are my customers' long-term goals and how can I help achieve them?
- What do my customers perceive as 'added value'? Have I asked them or am I making assumptions?
- What do I do to add value to the customer?
- How do I exceed my customers' expectations?

Monitoring and assessing market developments ('market sensing')

Keeping a close eye on market developments will help you spot where and how the organisation can improve. Think about the following:

- To what extent does an informed, dynamic view of the market guide your or your managers' actions?
- How effectively does customer information flow around the organisation?
- Does everyone have an accurate, consistent and shared understanding of customers? Do you know who they are and what they want?
- Is there an over-emphasis on gathering and measuring data at the expense of actually doing something about it? (This syndrome has been called 'data infatuation'.)
- How comprehensively do you monitor what the competition is up to?
- Is your business creative in the way it responds to customer data? What would improve it?

Segmenting your markets

1. Manage the segmentation of your customers and make sure you review the information regularly. Remember to:

  - analyse and identify the most profitable customers
  - establish criteria and a process for segmenting customers in future
  - assess the characteristics of each customer segment

2. **Explain the results of this segmentation. Use the information to improve awareness and understanding of customers. Discuss how best to target initiatives at the most profitable customers and how to manage the least profitable ones.**

Developing new products

- **Exactly what will make the product unique or valuable to customers?**
- **Which benefits will be used to sell the product?**
- **How, where and by whom will the product be sold?**
- **What is the pricing strategy?**

Strengthen customer relationships

Each member of your team can help to build your relationships with customers. To help the team do that:

- **review your team's roles and responsibilities. Are the needs of customers being addressed properly?**
- **assess their skills and development needs. Do people have the skills and experience needed to serve customers?**
- **review information systems: do you have the right information about customers and is it getting to the right people at the right time? Could it be improved?**
- **include customer issues as a regular item on the agenda at team meetings and implement a customer service suggestion scheme, rewarding helpful suggestions.**

It's worth remembering that customers and their perceptions are everything. There's no silver bullet for customer loyalty. For you to be successful, customers have to see your product as being significantly different from everything else out there and offering excellent value for money. If you can pull this off, customers will stay loyal, which reduces sales costs, and they'll often pay a premium price for your product to boot.

WHEN THINKING ABOUT CUSTOMERS, SALES AND BUSINESS DEVELOPMENT ISSUES, CONSIDER WHETHER YOUR BUSINESS

- focuses on delivering its customers a consistent, ideally 'branded' experience each time they deal with the business
- clarifies how, in the eyes of customers, it offers value
- provides incentives for new customers to return and reorder
- rewards loyalty for established customers
- emphasises the issues of greatest relevance to customers
- makes the customers' experience as easy and enjoyable as possible
- reassures customers with reliability
- uses customer feedback to improve processes and products
- understands that business, particularly on-line, is individual
- segments the market as simply as possible, ensuring segmentation is rational
- over-complicates any aspect of the business
- changes its product offer too frequently or stays the same for too long
- ignores problems and potential pitfalls
- focuses on internal divisions, products and its own view of the world
- focuses on appealing to its most profitable customer groups
- fails to communicate, both internally and externally

4 INCREASING REVENUE: MARKETING AND PRICING

Increasing business revenue is a constant challenge, but it's made even tougher during a downturn by competitive pressures, cash-flow challenges and other constraints. However, as with other business skills during a downturn, selling *well* is the key to weathering difficult times. Selling allows you to invest in products, resources and processes that enable you to sell more. During a downturn, the scarcity of one resource—such as customers to generate revenue or capital to invest in enhanced sales systems—makes selling, and increasing revenue, difficult.

The question to consider first is this: in your business, how might selling differ from increasing revenue? Let's say that selling means getting new customers or selling more to existing ones, whereas increasing revenue might mean increasing prices for items that are already 'sold', perhaps by offering a new feature with your product or service. Selling and increasing revenue are, of course, very similar and frequently, but not always, the same.

Increasing revenue *and* sales

Whatever the business and whatever its stage of development, increasing revenue requires two things: a focus on the right priorities; and an ability to influence attitudes and generate a favourable perception. These skills are the key to increasing revenue and surviving a downturn.

> Techniques to increase revenue can be deployed at any stage of organisational development. A 'climate of profitability' must be present right from the start.

It's important to understand early on the crucial issues affecting sales and revenue for your business or team. A new business will face different issues during a downturn from an established one. For example:

- **Do you need to show potential customers that your brand can be trusted?**
- **Do you need to reassure customers that the downturn has not harmed your product or service?**
- **How can you best use your name and reputation?**

Use this opportunity to update or improve your sales processes, systems and people. In what way can you make them more effective, or more inclusive? The more people you keep on board—whether they be investors, employees, local communities in areas where you manufacture and distribute, or customers—the better your chances of riding out the downturn.

Mastering marketing

A marketing plan is a vital tool in your campaign to increase revenue and sales during tough times. This useful document can help you to:

- **develop the strength and value of a brand**
- **match, deter or undermine competitors**
- **build customer loyalty**
- **launch a new product**
- **enter a new market with an existing product**
- **slow the decline of a specific product**

Developing a successful marketing plan requires careful consideration of a variety of issues; the most significant being:

1. **market segmentation**
2. **product knowledge and differentiation (what makes your business different or exceptional)**
3. **customers**
4. **competitors**
5. **pricing**
6. **sales strategies and techniques**

As with any plan, it needs to be as clear and simple as possible. Carry this clarity across to your sales approach: it has to be straightforward for customers and remove any obstacles to actually making the sale.

Market segmentation

As discussed in Chapter 3, market segmentation involves analysing groups of current and potential customers so that you can understand how the market is organised and what it's composed of, analyse related information, develop the effectiveness of marketing plans and target potential customers. Make sure your segmentation is focused; the larger a segment is, the greater the danger that it will lose value. The value of segmentation lies in highlighting differences and specific customer characteristics.

Product knowledge and differentiation

To market a product or service effectively, focus on its benefits, not simply its features, so that you can show how it *genuinely* compares favourably to competitors.

Understanding your customers

Knowing what your customers want enables you to match your product or services to their needs. This crucial point should underpin the whole marketing plan. For example, if your product has a niche market, keep this uppermost in your mind when you're making decisions about pricing or sales methods. Also:

- market research can help to put you in touch with customers in your target market. You can make it relatively formal, using detailed surveys or desk research, if you have the time or budget, but you can also do it informally. Often a simple discussion with current or potential customers is helpful when you're putting together the marketing plan.

- a feature/benefit analysis focuses on the product's attributes. For example, a computer may have a top of the range internal modem and the latest processor chip, features which are useful for getting people's attention.

Understanding your competitors

Knowing what the competition is up to is important, and it involves more than just a passing observation of their current activities. Think about:

- analysing what competitors have done, what they offer at the moment and what they may do in the future
- understand how they operate this way, and why
- assess their strengths: what is it that puts them ahead when competing with your business?
- understand their weaknesses: what is it about you and your business that is better? Perhaps this needs to be explained to customers.

Pricing and sales techniques are both central to the challenge of increasing business revenue, and are explored in detail below.

Pricing

Pricing is a surprisingly complex and important area of business, but it's often neglected. At first glance it appears a straightforward, almost mundane activity: you can either charge people what an item cost you to make plus an arbitrary mark-up, or else simply charge what you believe the market will bear. If in doubt, look at what your competitors are doing before you make your decision.

In reality, though, pricing is much more involved for many reasons, both direct and indirect. For example, pricing:

- **influences perception of the product and brand (a premium price may actually stimulate sales if it reinforces customer perception of quality, prestige or some other intangible factor, such as reliability)**
- **directly affects sales growth and customer loyalty**
- **is an important way of determining profitability**
- **is very difficult to change once fixed**

Despite its significance, business owners often make pricing decisions in the dark, relatively speaking. Rather than rush in and make an arbitrary decision, spend as much time as you can on thinking through the whole issue and its implications for *your* business: pricing is not only a major source of competitive advantage, but it also provides a way to:

- **increase loyalty to a brand or product**
- **enable firms to enter new markets**
- **sustain the life of an established product**
- **provide a vehicle for special offers and other sales techniques**

Let's put it this way: if the price is wrong, the business can collapse, or, at best, an opportunity is wasted. So how can you make sure that your pricing is working best for you?

Understand customer perceptions and behaviour

Knowing what the customer wants and expects are among the biggest issues underlying pricing. Successful pricing is based on a clear understanding of the specific needs and nature of the target market. The culture of the market will also affect pricing decisions; so, if there is an acceptance of a particular type of pricing structure or approach, it's likely that your pricing strategy will follow suit. The maturity of the market you're working in can also influence pricing: if the market is mature with relatively few new customers, pricing needs to concentrate on taking customers from competitors as well as retaining market share. However, if the market is new and growing, the aim then is to build and gain market share as rapidly as possible. These two approaches may or may not lead to the same result. Finally, if the market is declining, prices may need to be cut just to compete for the dwindling number of available customers.

Recognise your competitors

The competitiveness of the market clearly affects pricing decisions. If you don't have many competitors, you'll probably have a bit more leeway when it comes to making pricing decisions.

The nature of the competition is also important, as some competitors may be vulnerable to lower prices, especially if their costs prevent them lowering prices any further. Other competitors may be open to claims of poor value or quality. In this situation, a higher price accompanied by appropriate advertising could reinforce perceptions that your product offers premium value and quality. A useful rule is to target one competitor or a group of competitors, attacking them with the most appropriate pricing strategy.

Review costs and understand cost structures

This stage involves checking all of the direct costs of sales, which means understanding what they're comprised of. As well as checking costs charged by your suppliers, take account of other, less obvious costs that are directly attributable to the product, such as marketing and sales expenses, distribution costs or professional fees, such as accountancy. There is a tendency to categorise as many costs as possible as overheads and remove them from calculations of gross profit (which of course relies simply on revenue minus directly attributable costs of sales). When calculating gross profit, it is usually best to include any cost which varies in direct proportion to the size of sale. However, given the complexity of most business situations, often the best approach is to talk to your management accountant about direct and indirect costs. This will highlight the importance when pricing of going all the way to the bottom line (meaning net profit) to set the minimum price needed to break even for a given volume of sales.

Apply break-even analysis (cost-volume-profit or CVP analysis)

Break-even point occurs when sales cover costs, where neither a profit nor a loss results. It is calculated by dividing the costs of the project by the gross profit at specific dates, making sure to allow for overhead costs. Break-even analysis is used to decide whether to continue development of a product, alter the price, provide or adjust a discount, or change suppliers in order to reduce costs. It also helps with managing the sales mix, cost structure and production capacity, as well as forecasting and budgeting.

For break-even analysis to be reliable, the sales price per unit should be constant, as should the sales mix, and stock levels should not vary significantly.

View pricing from the buyer's perspective

If you can, test your understanding of the most important issues facing your customer. Whether in person or in the form of a written communication (such as a mailshot), you should make your customer feel important by relating your product to their key objective.

Choose the best pricing strategy

Once costs, market and product issues have been considered, the pricing strategy can be set. This involves deciding whether to follow the prevailing pricing trends or to follow a potentially riskier but higher return strategy of innovating using price. The type of pricing strategy (for example, loss leading or penetration pricing—see table overleaf) can also be varied, so that the plan is to offer one price in one market (to enable market penetration, for instance) and another, such as 'milking' or 'skimming', in a different one.

Dos and don'ts: pricing

Do

- **view pricing decisions from the customer's perspective**
- **consider how competitors may respond to pricing decisions**
- **try to build flexibility into the price, allowing room for distributors or sales people to provide special offers, for example**
- **cover your costs—all of them, now and in the future**

PRICING STRATEGY	WHAT IT IS	HOW IT WORKS
Loss leading	Selling a product at less than its cost in order to remove competitors or establish market share.	Loss leading is an unusual and even a desperate tactic. It *can* work at certain times, but it's risky. If demand

PRICING STRATEGY	WHAT IT IS	HOW IT WORKS
		rises too far too fast, so will the product's losses. Also, it can be a trap from which there is no easy escape, as customers will come to expect low prices and won't be happy when they're increased.
Penetration pricing	Combining a low price (break-even or slightly better) with aggressive marketing techniques to penetrate the market, rapidly establishing a presence and gaining a significant amount of market share.	Another high-risk strategy, this is especially suited to entering competitive markets or attacking established leaders in a specific market. The hope is that as demand rises, unit costs will fall and the whole exercise will work out. The danger is that competitors will reduce their prices; so if possible it is best to do it when competitors' prices are already low.
'Milking' or 'skimming'	Charging premium prices for top-quality versions of an	'Milking' involves selling an established product to a high-income market

PRICING STRATEGY	WHAT IT IS	HOW IT WORKS
	established, standard product.	and convincing that market of the advantages over the standard version. For example, a publisher might produce a hardback edition or perhaps a gold-embossed limited edition of a classic novel. In reality, large costs plus a smaller market often make this approach of limited value.
Price differentiation	Charging different prices for the same product in different markets, according to what customers are willing to pay.	This strategy enables the business to generate the most revenue from its product. However, it has its risks. It only works when there are barriers to entry, such as tariffs or high transport costs, that prevent wholesalers buying in low-price markets and reselling. It also relies on a measure of consumer ignorance or tacit

PRICING STRATEGY	WHAT IT IS	HOW IT WORKS
		acceptance of prices elsewhere. Examples include the different prices charged for CDs in different markets, and the widely varying sums charged in different European countries for the same model of car.
Target pricing	Fixing a price by targeting a minimum level of profit and estimating likely sales volumes at specific prices.	One of the most popular approaches to pricing, it does, however, rely on accurate estimates of sales volumes and it can tend to ignore competitors' actions.
Marginal cost pricing	Charging a price that reflects the extra cost to the company of supplying one extra item to a customer.	When the cost of one extra item varies significantly, this approach works, as for example when postage or parcel delivery rates vary according to location. But it does require an explanation as to why prices vary for essentially the same item.

PRICING STRATEGY	WHAT IT IS	HOW IT WORKS
Variable pricing	Reducing prices to stimulate business, or raising prices to deter business (if production capacity is full, for example).	This is a popular tactic in extreme situations, both to stimulate demand when sales are low and to deter it when sales are too high (it can happen!). The difficulties are in explaining the price fluctuations to customers, particularly when a reduced price must be raised.
Average cost pricing	Setting a base price by calculating total costs and the desired profit margin, and then dividing this total by likely sales volumes.	Together with target pricing, this is one of the most popular approaches to pricing and is most readily accepted by customers. It relies on accurate estimates, but it has the advantage of enabling firms with the lowest costs to charge the lowest prices.
Customary pricing	Charging the same price but reducing the contents of the package.	Because it is an attempt to increase profits by misleading customers, customary pricing risks

PRICING STRATEGY	WHAT IT IS	HOW IT WORKS
		incurring customers' resentment. It tends to happen when costs are rising and demand is slow.
Barrier pricing	Reducing prices to deter or remove new entrants to the market.	Barrier pricing happens in highly competitive or price-sensitive markets. It can take the form of a group of businesses in an industry collectively charging lower prices to deter new entrants. An aggressive strategy, it works when the company lowering its prices is defending a core market and is established (and wealthy) enough to sustain such an approach.

Don't

- rush into pricing without thinking about it carefully and doing plenty of research
- forget to consider timing when setting or altering prices
- forget that pricing can be a powerful sales technique— so decide which approach suits you best

■ **overlook future developments, from market changes
to supplier costs**

Improving sales techniques

Sales techniques are about developing a personal approach that is
bold, clear and sincere, using the sales person's individual skills
and abilities. The salesperson therefore needs to develop his or her
personal selling style in several ways. Good selling methods also
have to be appropriate for the market and the product.

Remember that selling:

1. **needs to be powerful *and* persuasive. It can involve
   highlighting the benefits of buying as well as the risks
   of not buying.**
2. **should be ethical. Avoid practices that will alienate
   customers and which aren't in their best interests:
   show your integrity, be attentive and sincere—or at the
   very least show that you understand what customers
   want and that you can relate to them.**
3. **requires an approach that sets the product apart from
   its competitors—a fresh, innovative approach will
   interest and motivate potential customers.**

Sales techniques that are particularly powerful include:

■ **direct selling,** in the form of key account management,
telephone selling and sales representatives who generate or
follow up sales leads.
■ **database and direct mail marketing.** This approach
enables customers to be targeted directly with sales
information and promotions with the greatest appeal. Some of

its benefits include being able to target offers selectively, test markets to make sure they're cost-effective, and being able to build up information about your customers' preferences and habits. The key thing here, however, is to make sure your customers actively welcome what you send them: if you're driving them mad with seemingly random or pointless letters and e-mails, all your efforts will end up in the bin.

■ **special offers.** These are a good way of launching new products and they can also regenerate interest in established ones. They provide a means of direct selling, and allow you to test products as well as gather detailed market intelligence. Offers are always appealing, but success may be short-lived if your customers are only interested in your product or service while the offer's on.

■ **Internet selling,** which appeals both to corporate and domestic markets. It's relatively easy, won't break the bank and can have an international reach too. Having said that, targeting the right customers can be difficult. Linking with other sites which potential customers may visit is vital.

Some of the following steps may also offer you a way to sharpen your sales focus and make it more effective.

Build a sales culture that generates increased revenues
Why not try:

■ **running an internal sales programme highlighting who your customers are (customer segments) and what they value, and the sales strategy**
■ **brainstorming ideas with team members to generate increased sales, and then prioritising each idea and assigning someone to make it happen**

- **reviewing how customer information flows round the business. Does it reach everyone in the team who needs to know about it? If it does, give people the opportunity to comment on it and ask them to suggest improvements and ways in which you can build on successes.**

> Customers' needs may vary, so tailor your messages to address this.

Review the effectiveness of past sales techniques

Not all sales techniques are equal. Rather than repeat past mistakes (or miss out on tried and tested useful options), think about:

- **which technique worked best?** Measure the marketing efficiency of each technique. To do this, divide sales revenue by marketing expenses. For example, if you spend £1,000 on marketing and generate £10,000 revenue as a result, your marketing efficiency is 10; for every £1 spent, £10 is generated.
- **why did it succeed?** This can be explained by focusing on customer segmentation.
- **review prices and discounts.** It could be that you're offering too large a discount or, on the other hand, your prices are too high for the market to bear. As noted above, price is a powerful sales tool: use it effectively. To gauge where you may be going wrong, why not organise a trial

offer to test out different approaches? It shouldn't be too expensive.

Measure how profitable your customers are

This allows you to focus your sales techniques in the most productive area and will help you work out how to sell items to customers: there's no 'one size fits all' approach that will work every time, so be ready to adapt your message to suit. At the same time it provides opportunities for selling complementary or extra products to existing customers (often referred to as 'cross-selling') and will also give you a way to develop what's known as a customer's 'lifetime value': in other words, the total value of their business to you. Measuring the profitability of both individual customers and customer segments will help to determine the structure, resources, direction and development of the sales effort, which means that your business will be able to develop its activities.

Gather customer feedback

You can do this by:

- **looking for opportunities to talk informally to customers**
- **following up on sales to see what happened after a sale**
- **exploring in detail why individual customers went elsewhere**

Meet customers directly

If you're the business owner, it's essential that you get out there to talk to your customers. If you have senior partners or colleagues, make sure they do too. When you meet customers, tell them all they need to know about the product or service you're selling, but make sure you keep the information in some type of context: don't just run through a rehearsed spiel if you can tell someone is in a rush, and don't pepper your speech with industry acronyms and jargon if the customer is new to your field.

If you lose the customer's attention, stop talking. Wait for him or her to speak, listen closely and show that you've listened by repeating a key idea or attitude in your own words. Deal with any questions that have cropped up and continue only when you're sure that the customer is satisfied and ready to listen.

Also, when you meet clients, ask for their order—this is best done without tricks or closing techniques: just ask! Look for buying 'signals' (such as nods of approval or a tendency to build on your ideas) and move straight to the order request.

Give customers more than they expect

By going just that bit further and surprising your customers (in a good way!), you'll find it easier to sell to them. It'll also be more likely that they'll pass on the good news to others and so generate potential new business. Once you know what your customers value, give them a bit more by:

- **keeping customers informed of how their order is progressing**
- **delivering before the agreed deadline**
- **saving customers time**
- **making things easier for customers—perhaps by delivering to their work rather than their home address**
- **personalising service**
- **giving customers peace of mind—offer them a money-back guarantee, for example**

Gain and maintain customers' trust

If your customers have confidence in you, you'll be selling from a privileged position that your competitors do not enjoy. To get your customers' backing:

- **view things from their perspective**
- **stick to your commitments**
- **build their loyalty to your business and respect for your brand (if there is something about your business that appeals to customers, find and develop it)**
- **close deals using a range of incentives that they actually value, such as discounts or easier payment terms**
- **act quickly and decisively to impress or reassure them. Hesitation, for whatever reason, may be interpreted as a lack of concern.**

Above all, when you are making changes or something goes wrong, tell customers what is going on and what you're doing to sort it out.

5 IMPROVING SALES AND THE SALES PROCESS

Selling involves communicating and negotiating, advertising and relating to people. Remember to study the market as well as body language: intuition and instinct are just as important to surviving a downturn as being clear and objective about your situation. For your business to succeed, you'll need to find out, by a variety of means, what your customers want and then give them a solution that matches their requirements. Good selling is about meeting needs in a mutually beneficial way; it is not about 'robbing' the customer.

Just as marketing relies on appreciating the 'marketing mix' (balancing product, price, place and promotion), an effective sales technique involves understanding, valuing and reaching customers. There are three core elements:

1. **understanding customers' needs.** The most common pitfalls in sales involve a lack of market awareness—in other words, being 'out of touch' with customers.
2. **increasing this need.** By increasing the customers' perceived need of a product or service, they progress along the 'value chain' and become of greater

commercial importance. Their perceived need may be influenced by complex variables, such as fashions and fads, or quality improvements brought by changes in technology.

3. **presenting the solution to this need.** In practice, this requires both the soft skills of influencing, negotiating and communicating, as well as the hard skill of a strategic understanding of the market. Above all, selling smarter requires both intelligence and high integrity; after all, you are working to understand someone's specific needs, which you are then trying to meet in a mutually beneficial way.

This chapter provides practical techniques to increase sales by doing the following:

- **managing the buyer's cycle**
- **strategic selling**
- **developing contacts and building rapport**
- **developing winning sales proposals**
- **making it easy for clients to buy**
- **succeeding at sales meetings**
- **creating customer motivation**
- **evaluating and improving team sales performance**

Managing the buyer's cycle

To understand how to sell, you have to understand how people buy. If you can appreciate how your offer is received, you will be able to improve how you sell your product or service. The whole process is known as the 'buyer's cycle'.

Awareness

Firstly, develop awareness of your business or new product among potential clients. This may provide a feeling of familiarity or comfort, or possibly alert interest or enquiry, and can then be used to lead customers into the next stage: information. The potential market size at this stage is 100%.

Information

Next, provide customers with specific details. Their interest may vary from a passing willingness to find out more to a passionate need to explore the offer. Whatever your customers' motives or situation, the information needs to be clear, useful and specific. Inevitably, the market size will have shrunk as some 'aware' customers fail to pick up the information, either through choice or circumstance.

Prioritisation

Customers will weigh up the benefits and then prioritise expenditure. For example, they may consider whether this is something they want to buy now, at this price and in this form. They may also evaluate alternatives. Clearly, some people will not make the move from having the information to prioritising a purchase.

Purchase

Having decided to buy, the next step for a customer is to complete the transaction. This stage in particular highlights the need for the buyer to be able to move as easily as possible through the process. Purchasing should be easy and satisfactory, and preferably enjoyable.

Use

This is a stage that is often forgotten, 'hidden' by the purchase. A sale isn't the end of the process, because customers have to use and value their purchase. If they don't, then the product may be returned, customers may stay away in future, and the future of the company's sales process may be adversely affected by poor publicity and a declining reputation.

Reuse

When the product or service (one of its components) is bought again, it not only generates additional revenue at a higher margin (without the cost of customer acquisition), but also shows customer loyalty to the product. It results in a stronger sales process, with more people moving into each stage.

Advocacy

Highly prized by sellers, this stage occurs when customers are so pleased with their purchase that they tell others about it, thus increasing awareness of the product or business and feeding back into the first stage of the process.

The rise of Dell Computer over the last two decades has been astounding, and it demonstrates the impact of the buyer's cycle. Dell's sales process is built on the principle that success comes to those who best understand the needs of potential customers.

The steps in the buyer's cycle are applicable to all types of sales, whether selling a product, service or idea by telephone or face to face, as an individual salesperson, as part of a team, or to internal clients and managers.

Buying attitudes are determined by the buyer's perception of the following:

- **the immediate business situation**
- **how your proposal is likely to change that situation**
- **the extent to which that change will close a gap or discrepancy between current reality and future goal**

Strategic selling

Selling and influencing require an interesting blend of art and science. Some aspects such as managing behaviour rely on 'softer' skills, for example, the ability to establish rapport, ask open questions and moderate levels of warmth and dominance. Other aspects require a focus on 'harder' skills, such as the need to fully understand each element of the sales process. Strategic selling brings together these soft and hard aspects into a coherent, co-ordinated and compelling approach.

> People will view your proposition from different perspectives. You need to understand the priorities of different groups involved in the sales process.

Define your unique sales objective

The first step when selling strategically is to be absolutely clear about what you are selling and the value it will bring. Be clear about what makes it an attractive proposition, and the value of your business to the organisation or client. This sounds simple but it is a challenge that can often become muddled or overlooked, with potentially disastrous consequences.

Identify all of the players in the buying cycle

These will include people that you may not know. Record their job title and name, if known.

Classify each of the players using the MATE model

This useful acronym highlights the need to focus on Money, Allies, Technical experts and End users.

The MATE Model

Money (ultimate veto)	**Allies** (unique and useful information, can guide you)
Technical Experts/ Assessors (filter out information, can be gatekeepers, can influence the money)	**End Users** (manage or work with your solution)

- **Money.** Who's the budget holder, with authority over the decision to spend? There is only one per sale; they tend to focus on the bottom line and they have the power of veto. They will probably ask 'What impact will this have and what return will we get?'

93

- **Allies** can help to guide you during the sales process. They provide valuable information, can lead you to the right people and may also be influential with decision makers. Allies are found both inside and outside the business and several people may play this role in a sale.
- **Technical experts** are 'gatekeepers' whose role is to evaluate technical aspects of the proposal. They do not have final approval but can offer recommendations to the decision maker. Also, they can say 'no' when it comes to technical issues. They will ask whether the product or service match their specifications.
- **End users** judge the impact of your proposal on their job performance. They will implement or work with your proposed solution; so there is a direct link between their success and that of the product. Because they have a direct interest they may also have some measure of influence in the decision to buy. Their issue is, 'Will it work for me or my department?'

Identify each player's influence over the buying cycle

Categorise their influence as high, medium or low and note areas requiring further investigation.

Consider the buyer's likely response

In particular, are they looking to gain from or prevent the sale? Are they feeling satisfied or arrogant?

Assess what results your proposal will give each person

What personal 'gains' or benefits will result? Results can be divided into corporate gains for the organisation as well as personal benefits for the individual.

Check for warning signs
Ask the following questions:

- **Have you at least one person for each area?**
- **Is there anyone whose influence you're not sure about? Have you made personal contact with them?**
- **Do you know they'll get back to you?**
- **Do you know what they would see as a good result or a 'win'?**

If you can't answer these questions fully, do some more research until you can. They're potential threats to the sale, otherwise.

Identify your tactics to further the sale and eliminate warning signs
Throughout this process you need to be honest and to be prepared to challenge and develop your thinking. With the information in place, the next challenges are to reach your key contacts, establish rapport and understand their needs.

Developing contacts and building rapport
Building relationships with key people is an essential part of any job. It is clearly important to develop your own style when networking, but there are several fundamental principles that can help.

Understand that honesty, openness and authenticity matter
People pick up on your values and motivations whether or not they are explicitly stated. Because of this, it really is important to be yourself, and to be open and positive.

Look for shared values
Such values may relate to work but could be to do with the wider community or environment, and may be important to people in their day-to-day lives.

Identify a shared mission or goal
Shared goals matter because people need to work in the same direction, demonstrating a commitment to goals beyond just their own personal priorities.

Use consensus, not force
Coercing someone implies that unless you exert pressure they won't fulfil their commitment or do the right thing. Trusting cultures are ones where people do things willingly. Clearly, developing proactive contacts and rapport can be achieved only with consensus.

Demonstrate a desire to learn, not blame
Again, this is linked to fear. In a culture of blame, people cannot trust others and be open. If people detect even a hint that someone will be blamed for something going wrong, trust and networks are destroyed.

Developing winning sales proposals
A sales proposal is the pitch you make to sell yourself, your products and services. It's about proposing a solution to a problem. A good sales proposal is a pitch that persuades a client to buy something they value, in a way that benefits you. Sales proposals happen more often than you might think. While a face-to-face meeting with a client is the traditional concept, a sales proposal is any opportunity you have to sell and can include, for example, a sales e-mail or

phone call. Winning with sales proposals is about maximising the opportunity that you have to increase sales revenue.

To sell anything requires that you tell the client what you can do. To be effective, you need to present yourself and your products, services and organisation well, using the techniques that enhance your sales pitch.

Sometimes, all that is necessary is to identify a potential client's needs and they will buy from you. At other times, the process is complicated by the need to let them know how you intend to meet their expectations and requirements. Rather than *tell* your client something, a successful proposal *sells* them something. Success here requires you to present a carefully planned, informed proposal to a client who is receptive to your ideas; information is critical.

Whatever form your sales proposal takes, and however you make the proposal, it is likely to consist of seven key stages.

1. **Getting yourself accepted.** Present yourself and communicate with your clients in such a way that they will want to hear the rest of your proposal. It is about body language, behaviour and, above all, promising something so attractive that clients will give you more of their time. If clients lack confidence in you, the rest of your proposal will be undermined.
2. **Stating your intent.** If you're clear about what your proposal will achieve and how it will solve their problems, customers will not only continue to give you their time, but also trust what you say.
3. **Asking the right questions that underline your USPs.** Don't just do what you've always done: question how your sales process works at the moment; are there problems that

need sorting out and that may be putting off your customers? Asking your customers for their opinion will help you pinpoint the gaps between how things are currently done and how they *could* be done, and in so doing underline your unique sales points.

4. **Checking you are addressing buyers' problems appropriately.** Before you can show clients how you can solve their problems, make sure that you know what their problems are. Check that you are on track and don't make any assumptions!

5. **Providing solutions to the buyer's problems.** This is the main part of your sales proposal. A sale is about addressing needs and persuading your clients that you can solve their problems by providing workable solutions. It is worth considering whether you are proposing alternative solutions to your clients' problems—presenting them with a choice—or demonstrating a single, compelling solution.

6. **Checking that your clients are happy.** You'll win umpteen brownie points by checking that you've addressed any concerns your clients have. If they've no queries, they'll still be pleased that you took the time to ask. If they do have some questions left, do all you can to deal with them there and then. If you can't answer everything, say you'll get back to them later that day or the next day if necessary, and keep to your promise.

7. **Closing the deal.** This stage takes place when your client is happy to accept your offer, but seeks to discuss the details. Delivery dates, quality parameters and opportunities for further business, for example, are all discussed when closing a deal.

The amount of time you spend on each of the stages of the above will, of course, vary from deal to deal. With brand new customers, it'll probably take a while for you to get accepted; at other times, it may be hard for you to address the buyer's problems or to negotiate over price when you are closing the deal. Always try to direct the potential buyer; a lack of direction makes you seem confused and distracts from your message. Several other techniques are also vital to ensuring the success of sales proposals.

Make a proposal to someone who can say 'yes'

If you make a proposal to sell something to a representative of an organisation who doesn't have the means or authority to buy, then no matter how good your proposal is, you won't get anywhere. Always propose to the person with:

- **means**
- **authority**
- **needs**

Whether or not you make them clear to the person listening to the proposal, be clear about your objectives.

Close effectively

Your proposal should work towards an effective close: you must remember to *ask for* the business. Once you have made a winning pitch, negotiate terms to go ahead. Your proposal process is not a regurgitation of your price list. Don't just win the proposal: win a longer-term relationship. During a downturn, there is a temptation to close quickly to secure valuable sales revenue. This is impatient and can cause problems long after you have pitched your proposal. A well thought-out close that benefits all parties is more valuable than an ill-planned or pushy one, chiefly because the relationship will be more positive in the future.

Handle objections

A feature of many sales proposals is the need to overcome objections raised by the prospective client (or 'prospect'). How you answer a question is far more important to the potential sale than the detail you give in the answer.

When dealing with objections, use the following structure:

1. **Acknowledge.** If you don't understand and empathise with the prospect's objection, you risk alienating them. It is better to work with, rather than against, them; stay on their side and find a solution that works.
2. **Ask.** Question what the nature of the objection is. Find out in detail about it, so you can come up with an intelligent solution. Not only will you be better able to persuade your client, but you will also be seen to have listened, which builds trust.
3. **Answer.** Proposing a convincing solution to their objection will bring the prospective client closer to buying. Having understood their problem, you will be able to produce a solution that is mutually beneficial.

Making it easy for clients to buy

Overburdening a client is a major pitfall when you're selling something, whether you're going through a downturn or not. If the client feels overwhelmed by information, they'll be (at best) resentful of your business and offer and almost certainly won't buy from you. Technology products suffer acutely from this: vendors often feel compelled to sell with a high degree of product detail that the vast majority of potential customers do not understand. To complicate matters, there are notable exceptions to this. High-performance cars, for instance, are often advertised with their technical specifications as a unique sales point (USP).

Decide what your USPs are, and be clear about them. The key to not overburdening a client with needless details is to understand what information they value and what they don't. Your USPs are what make the sale, nothing else, and communicating these effectively is all that is required to sell and increase revenue. USPs that are attractive and believable are what builds your brand in the long term.

Succeeding at sales meetings

The ability to understand and apply the seven step sales meeting process is one of the key differences between successful and less-effective sales people. The key stages that need to be mastered are as follows.

1. *Building rapport* to build credibility and create a constructive working relationship.
2. *Delivering a statement of purpose and potential benefit* enables you to gain control of the meeting, and to help the client appreciate the potential benefits.
3. *Introducing yourself and setting the agenda:* it is vital to explain who you are and why you are qualified to work with the customer.
4. *Fact finding* to help you to understand the business and the needs of the people involved.

5. *Exploring needs and wants* enables you to discover, at the necessary level, what this person really wants and what taking action would mean for them and the business.
6. *Presenting* to provide a tailored solution to meet your client's wants and needs.
7. *Advancing and closing:* two vital stages that are, in many cases, ignored altogether or handled poorly. In fact, if the preceding steps have been completed successfully, this is the logical conclusion: you will have earned the right to ask for the business.

Elements of the sales process can be applied in a wide range of situations. For example, developing rapport, stating your purpose and benefit and introducing oneself can be applied in meetings, negotiations and presentations, as well as sales situations. The skills, techniques and processes that are described below can also be used, at different times and in different ways, to influence others.

Building rapport

This is a vital aspect of sales meetings. Rapport is about quickly establishing common ground with your client and it's achieved through asking open questions, actively listening to and building on your client's answers. Using warm behaviour, open body language and smiling demonstrates professionalism and credibility. Appearance, body language and interaction will all be interpreted subconsciously by the potential client.

Open questions, which encourage customers to give information, usually start with 'who', 'how', 'what' or 'where'.

Professional sales people build rapport by asking open questions linked to three key topic areas:

- **personal ('How are things?', 'Did you have a good weekend?')**
- **situational ('What a great location! Why did you choose to come here?')**
- **business ('What key projects are you working on?', 'How's your new job?')**

In *How to Win Friends and Influence People*, Dale Carnegie highlights several ways to establish rapport quickly:

- **smile and be genuinely interested in other people**
- **remember that a person's name is the most important sound to that person**
- **be a good listener; encourage others to talk about themselves**
- **talk in terms of the other person's interests**
- **make the other person feel important, and do it sincerely**

Delivering a statement of purpose and potential benefit

Once the introduction has come to a natural conclusion the purpose of the meeting or phonecall needs to be communicated smoothly and succinctly. Having built a rapport you can move on to the next stage of the sales process, stating why you are here and the potential benefit for both parties.

It is crucial to make a strong statement of purpose and potential benefit to set the tone of the meeting, to earn the right to ask questions and to communicate professionalism. The 'potential' benefit (potential, because there is no guarantee at this stage that you can help) puts forward an answer to the client's 'What's in it for me?' (WIIFM), so that they are open-minded at this stage. Selling relies on the ability to make the client interested and engaged at each stage of the process, and to develop a professional working relationship. A good question to end with is: 'What are your expectations from today's meeting?'

Introducing yourself and setting the agenda

Once you've established a mutually agreeable basis for the meeting, the next stage is to introduce the company and agree an agenda. Although this is optional, depending on the stage of the relationship and the knowledge the client has, it is a good idea to introduce your company or business unit (if dealing with colleagues in the same organisation). The best sales people have a succinct, forceful introduction, which may include the background of the company or the business unit and their specialist area, including how they have helped other clients.

Fact-finding

Next, the professional sales person begins to find facts about the organisation and the potential client. Fact-finding enables the sales person to build a picture of the organisation that helps to identify areas of opportunity to discuss in more depth during the meeting. It requires the use of two key skills: open questions and active listening. Questions that a sales person might ask typically focus on the customer's products and clients, financial information, business challenges and strategy, competitors and markets and decision-making processes. You could ask:

- *Who* are your major clients?
- *How* is your business structured?
- *Where* are your major markets?
- *What* are the key challenges you are facing?

There are several key points that are essential to mastering this stage. First, different products require different background information. Make sure you obtain all the necessary information that you will need to present your product. Also, note the soft facts that you have picked up during the rapport about the person and their personality. These will be valuable later in personalising the benefits.

It is helpful to be succinct and enthusiastic when gathering this information: do not let the meeting lose its warmth and rapport. Once you have gathered the necessary information choose an angle to start exploring; you will know your product and spot the potential sales opportunities.

It is imperative not to start talking about the product or solutions at this stage. The fact-finding stage means understanding information about the client that is not easily available from other sources.

Exploring needs and wants

This is an essential, pivotal part of the sales process. It's vital because it informs *what* you offer as well as how and when you present it. So far, during the initial part of the meeting, the professional sales person has been:

- **establishing rapport to build trust and credibility**
- **introducing the purpose and benefit of the meeting to provide a clear objective**
- **asking open questions to discover facts about the client's business**

The final stages of presenting, advancing and closing follow naturally if the preceding stages have been successful. If this is the case, it's fine to say something like 'I think our product can help you, because ...'. Then, having linked the benefits with what you have already heard, ask customers what they think. If they agree that your product meets their needs, ask them for the business; if they don't agree, return to the fact find, explore their needs and improve the way you match your product to meet their needs.

Evaluating and improving team sales performance

To improve your team's sales performance, make sure you understand your current sales situation and can identify your strengths and weaknesses. Sales performance can be ascertained by analysing data, which represent 'key performance indicators'. The areas where they are most useful include:

- **the performance of your sales team or account managers**
- **loyalty**
- **opportunities**
- **costs**
- **countering competition**

Be aware of and clear about how your business measures, evaluates and develops performance remembering that the actual ratios are specific to the market in which you are engaged. For example, ratio analysis supports decision-making and enables leaders to monitor their actions and to avoid inappropriate or damaging actions. A ratio is simply a relationship between two numbers, but when compared to the same ratios for previous periods they can show important trends and patterns in performance. When using ratios ask the following questions:

- **Which ratio is most appropriate?**
- **What is the trend: how is the ratio developing and why?**
- **How reliable is the data on which the ratio is based?**
- **What comparisons are desirable in using a ratio?**

Where did it go wrong?

One practical activity to improve your sales technique is to focus on why a pitch didn't work out. This doesn't mean blaming anyone for the proposal not being taken on, but more positively, looking at what you and your team can do next time to improve your chances of success. Ask yourself:

- **Was there one big reason why the pitch failed?**
- **What was the relationship like with the customer before the pitch failed?**
- **When did you realise the pitch had failed?**
- **What could be done differently next time?**

One important way of improving the technique both you and colleagues in your sales team use to sell is to ask critical questions about your sales activities. This will raise your self-awareness and highlight areas for development.

- Do people in the organisation view sales from the customers' perspective, understanding how and why they buy? How well does the business know each individual customer?
- Do people in the organisation share information and insights about customers?
- Are product benefits (not simply product features) highlighted?
- What is the best way to appeal to customers? How should the product be sold? Is a simple, consistent and compelling message being used to sell the product?
- Does the firm measure the profitability of customers? Is the firm targeting, attracting and retaining the most profitable customers?
- Could you sell more to existing customers? How do you plan to keep customers loyal? Are your activities appealing to customers and difficult for competitors to copy?
- Do you have measures (aside from sales volume and revenue) to highlight your sales team's effectiveness?

As with leadership and business success in general, surviving a downturn requires the ability to keep several different tasks and priorities in balance simultaneously. As well as increasing revenue and developing sales, you'll also need to keep a very close eye on costs, as explained in Chapter 6.

6 CONTROLLING COSTS AND CASH FLOW

Whether or not businesses generate income, they generate costs. Whatever your objectives, you'll need to achieve them with a limited amount of cash, and sometimes you'll need to cut costs radically if the business is going through tough times. Despite its central importance to profitability, cost reduction is often done carelessly (even desperately), rather than effectively and rationally.

On a similar theme, it's essential that you keep a close eye on your finances. Cash and profit are the twin financial pillars on which a business survives, but many business owners and managers make the fatal mistake of focusing solely on profit, ignoring the fact that cash is the life-blood of the business. Knowing how much cash will be needed is particularly important for new businesses and smaller organisations; it is a key aspect of the overall business plan, not only for keeping on track but for gaining and maintaining the support of stakeholders such as shareholders and banks. The most fundamental of all financial statements, particularly for small and medium-sized businesses but also highly relevant to large companies, is the cash-flow forecast.

Businesses are more competitive, more flexible and stronger if costs are actively controlled and, above all, if in the organisation there is a culture of cost control. In particular, cost control and cash management mean that the business is better able to drive increases in revenue, take customers from competitors, enter new markets, develop new products and weather potential problems. What matters is not simply having 'low' costs (or relatively low costs compared to competitors) but having the right cost structure so that the business is generating profits, becoming more competitive and increasing in value.

Controlling costs and cash flow

Plan to control costs

You can do this in several ways:

- **Know what costs you control by understanding what you have budgeted to spend under each of the cost headings. The major areas of business expenditure include employment, materials, fixed and variable costs, overheads, production, administration, marketing, sales and professional fees.**
- ***Develop key performance indicators and actively monitor costs.* Make sure that you receive detailed information about costs, and the relationship between costs and profitability especially. You need to have quick access to the right information under each cost heading. Also, decide how frequently you will monitor costs.**
- **Make sure that members of your team know the areas of cost that they influence and how much is available to spend.**

Encourage people to find savings

Don't worry, you *can* do this without weakening the business. First of all, ask the people who actually spend the money for suggestions about how costs might be reduced. Is it time you took a good look at the terms you get from your suppliers, say? Do you really need to tie up so much money in stock? Next, show your team how important cutting costs is by linking cost reductions to things that they want (such as more money to spend on marketing or equipment) or by structuring reward systems to encourage it. Why not give a person who cuts costs by X amount or X% (fill in the gap with your business in mind!) an extra day's holiday?

Find out why costs rise

If costs have risen beyond budget, get to the root of it. It may be that the over-run was completely unavoidable—a piece of machinery may have given up the ghost, for example—but it's important that everyone in the business learns something from it so that (if possible) you can try to avoid it in future.

Keep budgets under tight control

Often, budgets are used merely to assess performance. Their real value, however, is as an active tool that can help you make sensible financial decisions. Try to see budgets in perspective and don't cut them rashly before you've thought through the knock-on effects.

Get paid quicker

Invoicing and receiving prompt payment from customers is vital for effective cash management. It can be a complex area, linked with many other aspects of the business, notably sales, but some of the key elements include:

■ **improve invoicing.** Whether you look after the invoices yourself or you have an accounts team to do the work, make sure that all invoices are dispatched as soon as possible: the quicker they go out, the quicker you'll get paid. They should be clear to the recipient, accurate and state when payment is expected. Include all relevant information on the invoice, such as customer order reference (if there is one), supplier's VAT number and delivery address. If appropriate to your business, you could investigate interim invoicing, whereby the business charges for work done to date, even if the project is not completed. This is particularly useful when selling professional services (such as legal and accountancy fees), where the work tends to happen over a long period of time. You must agree this type of invoicing at the outset of your working arrangement, however.

■ **encourage prompt payment.** In the future, legislation may be introduced forcing businesses to settle their debts within a fixed period, otherwise the supplier is legally entitled to charge interest. This seems some time away at the moment, however, but in the meantime suppliers can encourage prompt payment by offering a discount on the current invoice or a reduction of the next, if payment is received quickly (say, within seven days). Clearly, make sure that the level of discount matches up with the size of the order and don't get carried away! It's best not to do this too often, as your customers may get used to it and just expect a discount as a matter of course.

■ **take up credit references.** Do everything you can to avoid bad debts or businesses that will probably need a nuclear detonation in order for them to pay. Checking creditworthiness is one way of doing this. As a minimum, when you deal with any business for the first time, get a bank and a trade reference.

- **impose credit limits.** It's a good idea to agree with sales staff a sensible level of credit that will be granted to customers—you can then extend (or reduce) this as the relationship with the customer develops (or deteriorates!). Clearly, a simple, effective system needs to be put in place by finance staff which alerts the relevant people (perhaps in sales or production) to the fact that a customer has reached their credit limit.

- **consider advance payment/ deposit with order.** For expensive or custom-made products or services (or for first-time customers), think about a policy of cash with order. You'll need to balance this approach against the likelihood of some people declining to work with you if they don't want to pay up front, but it's certainly worth a toe in the water.

- **collect late payments.** Make sure that there's one person in your business who's responsible for collecting overdue payments, and that he or she has an effective process for doing this. For example, on the day that payment is due, send a letter with all the relevant details of the outstanding invoice to the person who placed the order. Ring seven days later if you don't hear anything. If either of these steps yield any queries, make sure they're addressed and resolved straightaway so that there are no further excuses for holding up the payment. If neither approach works, the next step is a final letter, warning of the consequences of failure to pay—legal action—and stating the date after which it will be taken.

An alternative approach is simply to factor out the debt, so that another company pays you a percentage, undertaking to recover the debt themselves. You do have to pay for this service, though, and factoring doesn't work for every business, so mull it over carefully.

■ **consider matching your financial systems to your markets.** It can help to decide who you do *not* want to sell to, and then to organise your systems to effectively exclude these groups. For example, direct selling overseas is often expensive for certain businesses once the cost of carriage and exchange rates have been accounted for, added to which are the element of risk and the difficulties in recovering overdue payment. The solution might be to insist that overseas customers pay in advance at a fixed exchange rate and are responsible for the delivery costs. This is one method of avoiding bad debts, although it can also be a way of avoiding sales! The approach usually works for occasional orders to markets that are neither the core of the business nor present any immediate opportunity.

Manage stock levels

Recent surveys estimate that the cost of holding goods in stock can be anything up to 35% of the value of the goods themselves. So, £100,000 worth of stock can cost £35,000 to hold in stock for a year. Additional costs include: interest for the goods and their storage; insurance; theft and wastage; stock handling costs for staff and equipment, and warehouse or rental costs. Costs of this kind can be avoided by establishing an efficient process for just-in-time (JIT) production, perhaps passing some of the risk on to other businesses in the supply chain. Also, it is important that there is effective communication between staff in production, purchasing, sales, marketing and finance. For example, sales and marketing personnel need to tell production and purchasing of likely campaigns and potential increases in business.

Manage purchasing and creditors

This needs to be completed efficiently, without incurring any direct or indirect penalties. It is worth considering the following techniques:

- **make the most of your purchasing power by planning the likely volume of business and by using a select band of suppliers. In this way, lower prices or extended payment terms may be agreed.**
- **set up secure and efficient procedures for authorising expenditure and payment**
- **keep an eye on the time taken to pay creditors: never assume that they are much less important than customers and can be treated poorly. If they are, they can take action that may reduce the success of your organisation.**

Focus on major items of expenditure

Classify costs as either 'major' or 'peripheral'. Often, undue emphasis is given to the 80% of activities accounting for 20% of costs, rather than focusing on those activities that generate the most costs.

Increase cost awareness

Casualness is one of the pitfalls of cost control. While it's clearly important to focus on major items of expenditure, you can still cut the cost of smaller items too. One good way of cutting costs over the medium to long term is to influence people's attitudes towards cost and wastage. Look at your own attitude to cost control and reduction: can your staff see you actively looking for and putting into practice cost-control measures? You have to show a good example here and encourage everyone to spend more wisely.

> Cost control relies on a positive attitude to budgeting. People need to understand, accept and use the budget, feeling a sense of ownership and responsibility for it.

Balance costs and quality
Commercial management and cost control means getting the best value possible. This requires a balance between price paid and quality received.

Use budgets to help you actively manage finances
Budget early so that the financial requirements are known as soon as possible. Consider the best time-period for the budget—normally a year, but it depends on the type of business. Budgets can be of interest to others outside the normal running of the business, as well as providing a starting point for cash-flow forecasts. They are also useful in monitoring costs.

Cut out wastage
For decades, leading Japanese companies have directed much of their cost management efforts towards *muda* 'waste elimination',

which involves techniques such as process analysis, mapping and re-engineering, and these are important parts of operational decision-making. By thinking of activities as a chain of events from the beginning of the process to the end, with each part of the chain comprising discrete, identifiable tasks, process analysis enables waste to be identified and eliminated and costs to be reduced.

Manage overheads

It's always a good idea to plan expenditure on overheads (such as office costs or new equipment), but incurring expenditure *too soon*—that is, before the increased activity happens—is one of the most common causes of cash flow problems. Caution and timing are essential, and the key to success is to delay new costs for as long as possible without jeopardising the business.

Keep people informed

Make sure that every single external party concerned with the financial well-being of your company—bankers, shareholders and advisers such as accountants—are kept informed of major plans and developments. If any difficulties do crop up, it'll be much easier for them to understand how the situation has arisen and to offer their support than if they're unfamiliar with the business in general and the management in particular.

Avoiding problems with costs and cash flow

- **Do all that you can to make sure that customers pay as quickly as possible.**
- **Control fixed, overhead costs at a level that can be routinely sustained by the business.**
- **Manage stock levels closely to avoid all your cash being tied up in it.**

- Keep open lines of credit: this means talking regularly to financial backers (especially banks), keeping them informed of your plans and situation, and having enough sources of finance available (for example, overdraft and loan facilities).
- Regularly forecast cash flow, during good times and bad, and improve cash-flow forecasting.
- Let everyone in the business know how vital it is to control cash and costs.
- Rigorously analyse major expenditure decisions and understand the cash-flow implications.

Key questions: focusing on costs and cash flow

- Do you know the biggest areas of cost for your business, both in real terms and percentage growth?
- Where are costs escalating, where *might* they escalate and what is the cause?
- Are people rewarded for actively reducing costs? Can you give them an incentive to do it?
- Who are your major suppliers? Have you discussed with them how your costs (their prices) might be controlled or reduced? Is it time for a change?
- Have you prepared a cash-flow forecast?
- Do you monitor how much cash is in the business, striking a balance between keeping and investing cash?
- When investing cash, is the business aware of the time value of money—the fact that money now is worth more than the same sum of money in the future?

Dos and don'ts: costs and cash flow

Do

- find out why costs have risen above budget
- act quickly to curb unplanned cost increases
- compensate for overspend by cutting back in other areas if you can't reduce rising costs
- keep people informed of costs, whether they are rising, falling or stable, and advise on what action is being taken to keep costs on target
- encourage people to reduce costs and eliminate waste
- make sure that your team members appreciate the time value of money
- prepare and monitor two financial statements: the budget and cash-flow forecast

Don't

- ignore cost over-runs
- fail to raise awareness of cost issues
- assume that because sales are being generated cash is flowing: a sale is not made until the cash is received, and so you need to understand your debtors and their capacity to pay on time
- ignore debtors, creditors or suppliers—they all need to be carefully managed and monitored

Using a cash-flow forecast

Forecasting the cash needs of a business is essential: you must have a clear idea of how much cash will be required for the business to run and develop effectively. Bear in mind these vital points when you're preparing and using a cash-flow forecast.

Structure the cash-flow forecast

The cash-flow forecast needs to be structured in a table, with receipts and payments set against the month that they occur, showing the flow of money in and out of the business. The forecast is divided into three separate sections:

1. **Receipts and money coming into the business. This includes cash, debtors and loans.**
2. **Payment, including trade creditors, wages, overheads, equipment, loan repayments, overdraft interest, staff costs and tax.**
3. **Balances: monthly as well as cumulative balances.**

Prepare the forecast

When you prepare the forecast, you'll probably need to prepare a budget for the business for the year ahead. The first step is to fill in regular payments that you can predict (such as staff salaries, rent, utility bills). Next, estimate likely sales revenues; include the time when the cash will be *received*, not when it will be invoiced. From the sales forecast you can then calculate and include the costs of sale and the direct costs (such as raw materials) that are related to the levels of sales and production. Finally, remember to include figures for the month in which they will *actually* be received or paid.

Use it!

After spending so much time putting together this useful document, don't let it gather dust. Use it to work out a number of things, including how much cash the business needs; when you might need additional cash (for example, in the form of loans); what you can afford to spend (for example, on staff costs). Don't be overoptimistic when you're anticipating cash flows, especially when you're starting up.

Keep an eye on cash flow

Prepare a rolling cash-flow forecast, updated at the end of each month and looking at the next three months. The tighter the control of cash needed, the shorter the forecast period should be. If money is really tight (as it probably will be during a downturn), it may be worth doing a rolling weekly forecast for the next month. In addition, comparing actual receipts and payments with the forecast will help to refine the forecasting process and highlight differences that may need to be accounted for later.

7 LEADING YOUR BUSINESS THROUGH A DOWNTURN

Leadership is a complex, multi-faceted activity that is all-consuming, except that during a downturn it can suddenly become much simpler. In difficult or challenging circumstances, what matters most is leadership that is active and focused. Several issues, are essential—building trust, using intuition, and developing personal effectiveness—and we'll look at those in this chapter. Arguably the most significant challenge, however, is to establish a clear, compelling vision that guides and energises people.

Establishing a clear, compelling vision

Think of vision as the destination, not the journey. The means of transport and the route you take will change depending on circumstances, but you know where you are going. Because things can change so much (and so often) during a downturn, it's not always helpful to set goals based on short-term activities and prescribed ways of working—no sooner have you defined what you want than the plan changes! By keeping focused on the destination, though, you're more likely to stay on course and accept change, even when shifting circumstances require a different approach.

A clear, guiding vision is what defines successful leaders, sustaining them through good times and bad. This type of vision is essential because it:

- **inspires others and generates commitment**
- **provides a clear focus for action**
- **establishes a set of values to guide actions and channel efforts**
- **builds confidence, guiding decision-making, problem solving and innovation**
- **fosters teamwork and ensures consistency**

A guiding vision

This can be developed and applied at several levels. It needs to support, integrate and align with the overall vision of the organisation.

TYPE OF VISION	PURPOSE AND VALUE	CHARACTERISTICS
Overall vision for the organisation	• provides a clear direction and aspiration for the business • inspires, mobilises and engages people • guides behaviour and decisions at all levels (providing a starting point for other business visions)	inspiring and aspirational, clearly setting the direction, tone and priorities for the whole organisation as well as informing customers and shareholders

TYPE OF VISION	PURPOSE AND VALUE	CHARACTERISTICS
Business unit, department or team vision	• provides a clear, guiding direction for the business unit, department or team • supports the overall vision by translating it into a realistic aspiration for the smaller team, sustaining commitment and energy	inspiring and directly relevant to the work of the team, it engages and mobilises people so they work together, contributing to the overall success of the business
Individual or task vision	• provides a clear focus for action in a specific area or for a particular task • used when delegating, or when forming or reforming a team	guides the way that the task or role is approached, ensuring a clear view of what success will look like

Key questions: establishing a compelling vision

■ How clear and effective is the vision for: your organisation? Your business unit or division? Your team?

■ How compelling and engaging is your vision? How do people (employees, shareholders and customers) feel about the strategy?

■ Do you use a vision when setting objectives or delegating?

- Do people accept your vision and use it to guide their actions? How can you improve this, or get them to keep up the good work?
- How would you describe the values of your organisation? Does everyone in the organisation understand and recognise these values? Are they reflected in the way that people work?
- Do you understand and value your current business strategy and how it differentiates your organisation from its competitors?

Establishing the corporate vision

How this is achieved depends on your style. Some leaders prefer to find a consensus, while others are more directive and voice their own vision. Think about what would be the most effective, flexible and profitable direction for your business to take and then:

- decide which factors matter most. Are you looking for long-term success or short-term survival? Would you like to adapt the business to likely changes, transform it to be more profitable, customer-focused, pioneering, risk-averse—or something else?
- explain the need for a clear vision to everyone in the business so that they can contribute to the process from their own perspective.

Developing a guiding vision

A vision can be used to direct behaviour at any level, not simply to achieve your business's main goals but also to guide how a piece of work will progress, or what successful completion of a specific task will look like. It needs to be:

- clear and unambiguous so that everyone understands what is needed
- aspirational—motivating people and making sure they're committed to the planned outcome
- detailed and relevant enough to guide the way people work

Communicating the vision

For a vision to have greatest value, it needs to be shared and accepted and to gain the understanding and commitment of managers and influencers. If you can get everyone to agree to your vision, you'll all fulfil it much more quickly. When you're trying to get your message across to others:

- use powerful and emotive language and images to mobilise people
- explain what is needed and what factors should guide their actions (ideally in order of priority)
- don't be patronising and over-simplify your vision, or conversely, assume too much knowledge

Using the vision

The vision needs to guide actions and plans across the organisation and at all levels. Leading by example will demonstrate how your decisions and actions are influenced by it. Examples of early successes help to gain support for the vision, which will gather momentum and can be steadily reinforced by further success stories and news of initiatives, so that its influence becomes constant.

Your vision must be clear and appealing. How will it be perceived? How will it be organised? What will be different about it? Paint a clear picture of what the future will look like. It must excite and inspire as many people as possible.

Leading change in your business

It is often said that the only constant in business is change. The task of initiating, directing and controlling change falls to the leader, and there are several techniques that contribute to success. The eight-stage process of creating major change was first outlined by John Kotter in his bestselling book *Leading Change*; it describes what the leader needs to do to ensure that beneficial change is achieved.

Establish a sense of urgency

As a leader, you should initiate or take control of the process by emphasising the need for change. The more urgent and pressing the need, the more likely it is that people's attention and commitment will be focused. Usually the leader's role is to stay positive and build on success. However, at this time it actually helps to emphasise failure: what might go wrong; how, when and what the consequences could be. This can include examining market pressures and competitive realities and it may also involve identifying and discussing crises or potential crises.

Create a 'guiding coalition'

You'll need a team of people best placed to get you through the mire the business is in: this team is often referred to a 'guiding coalition'. The guiding coalition needs to understand very clearly what you want it to achieve so that it doesn't get off on the wrong foot. The group should be united, co-ordinated and carry significant authority in the organisation. It needs to have the power to make things happen, fundamentally changing systems and procedures where necessary, but it also needs the respect of people so that they'll 'buy in' to its ideas.

Develop a vision and strategy

As the business owner or manager, you and the guiding coalition need to create a simple, powerful vision that will direct and guide the change and achieve the goals required. Following that, concentrate on creating a detailed strategy for achieving that vision that is:

- **practical and workable on an operational level**
- **understandable and simple**
- **consistent across the business (one area's strategy should not undermine another elsewhere)**

Make sure that you communicate the vision clearly to everyone. Doing this persuasively will make sure that everyone understands what needs to be done, get the ball rolling and energise the team into tackling the issue at hand.

Encourage everyone in the business to act

For a business to change, everyone has to pitch in, not just the owner and any managers there may be. To get the best from your people, allow them to work in a blame-free and supportive environment. To empower them:

- **remove obstacles in the organisation**
- **change systems or structures that undermine the change vision**
- **encourage risk-taking and non-traditional ideas**

Generate short-term wins

Short-term wins are valuable in managing change because they highlight what is required and what the process means, they generate momentum for change and provide an opportunity to build on success. To do this, you should therefore:

- **plan for visible improvements in performance, or 'wins'**
- **create those wins**
- **visibly recognise and reward people who make the wins possible**

Consolidate gains and produce more change

This part of the process is the hardest: the excitement of the start-up phase has passed, successes have been built and people know what is needed, but now they are tired and problems and difficulties still arise. The key is to move steadily: maintain momentum without moving too fast and destabilising the process. Inevitably it will take time. You need to continue by:

- **using increased understanding of what is needed to change systems, structures and policies that don't fit the transformation vision**
- **hiring, promoting and developing people who can implement the change vision**
- **reinvigorating the process with new projects, themes and agents of change**

Develop a trustworthy leadership style

In a downturn, several leadership activities are vital and can easily be overlooked.

Confront people without being confrontational

We trust someone whom we can rely on to tell us the truth. Many leaders fail to do this because they are afraid that they won't be able to handle someone's reaction; they are afraid of hurting their feelings, they want to be liked, or they simply feel uncomfortable about having that kind of difficult conversation. The problem is that if we don't know what the leader really thinks we are forever reaching in the dark.

Therefore, an important part of the leader's integrity is to be honest, open and frank, without being aggressive or hostile. Richard Reed of the Innocent Drinks Company believes people trust him as a leader because he 'won't deviate from harsh reality, no matter how bad the news is'. He says that the management team members are close friends and that helps. 'We know each other inside out and we can be painfully honest with each other ... we don't hide behind anything, we know each other's strengths and flaws and we are totally open and honest.'

Admit when you don't know

Trusted leaders are able to talk about their vulnerabilities or admit when they are wrong. We tend to be suspicious of people who act as though they have all the answers. People who think they are right all the time won't be trusted because they are deluding themselves as well as others.

Many leaders believe that they should have all the answers and that it is a sign of weakness if they don't. It's hard for them to admit they don't know. The important thing for leaders is that they know what they want to achieve, that they have a vision. They can't possibly know enough about everything needed to achieve that vision. Sometimes they too may make mistakes or get it wrong.

Do the right thing and the money will follow

Measurement and focus on profit are vital, but too many companies focus on it to the detriment of attending to other things that drive profit, like employee and customer satisfaction. In the words of Richard Reed from Innocent: 'We don't want to please our customers; we aim to infatuate them. We are doing what we care about. It's a cause, not a profit line.'

Understand the connection between trust and innovation

A culture of trust enables people to take risks and come up with ideas that they are passionate about. What If? is a UK-based company that teaches its clients how to make their businesses more innovative. Their processes challenge people to see things differently by stepping out of their comfort zone and to risk saying something that may seem counter-intuitive. They highlight two separate processes needed for innovation. One is idea building, where people come up with ideas, build and nurture them; the other is where these well-formed ideas are subject to analysis.

Companies that struggle to be innovative often do so because ideas get trampled by the force of judgement and analysis. Having the right kind of processes for idea generation and innovation is important, but processes are not enough. Innovative organisations are so because they also have an environment and culture that support and foster innovation.

So, what are the characteristics of successful innovators? They include:

- awareness—each person knows the goals of the organisation and believes he or she can play a part in achieving them

- **multiplicity**—teams and groups contain a wide and creative mix of skills, experience, background and ideas
- **connectivity**—relationships are strong and trusting and are actively encouraged and supported within and across teams and functions
- **accessibility**—doors and minds are open; everyone in the organisation has access to resources, time and decision makers
- **consistency**—commitment to innovation runs right through the organisation and is built into processes and leadership style

'Leadering' in a time of change
Build and maintain trust

Trust, which is always important, matters immeasurably during a downturn and in challenging or uncertain circumstances. Communication is one way to establish or build trust between yourself and your colleagues, customers and other stakeholders. Trust is essential to the manager's credibility.

Research among employees in Europe, the USA and Asia found that when deciding whether to trust someone the top ten most popular attributes are:

1. fairness
2. dependability
3. respect
4. openness
5. courage
6. unselfishness
7. competence

8. supportiveness
9. empathy
10. compassion

These are *the drivers of trust.* Understanding and delivering each of these qualities is vital if trust is to be developed.

Trust is recognised as being fragile and tricky to build; so it should come as no surprise if this list appears demanding. To succeed, consider how, in practical terms, you build trust. What do you do to establish credibility?

Show moral courage

Being consistently courageous means different things to different people, but above all it implies an ability to do and say what you mean, especially when faced with adversity. It also requires a capacity to take risks, to be constant and determined, to admit mistakes and to stand alone when necessary. Courage is a quality that is universally respected; even if we do not agree with a particular idea or approach, we admire bravery and the associated qualities of integrity, conviction and determination. Moral courage, the courage of our convictions, is present in those people that we choose to trust.

Be dependable

Dependability develops trust, because co-operation and collaboration are often integral to it; people are encouraged to support each other with practical help and good communication as well as in other ways such as mentoring or sharing best practice and experience. Dependability also has something in common with other attributes of trust, such as unselfishness, fairness and compassion. Like them, it can mean giving up things—information, time, resources, pet projects—to help others succeed.

Develop your credibility

Credibility is rarely built or lost in an hour or a day, although it will be affected by initial perceptions of your actions. For example, are you consistent? Do you put into practice what you say? Do you display integrity in your attitudes and actions? Consciously and unconsciously, people will be analysing your words and actions. Once an opinion is formed, it will be very difficult to change.

There are no easy routes to establishing credibility: much depends on the organisational culture, experiences and circumstances. Leaders are seen as credible when they are

- **demanding but reasonable**
- **accessible and friendly but not too familiar**
- **decisive but thoughtful**
- **focused, but flexible**
- **dynamic without being overwhelming or distracting**
- **tough and determined but fair and realistic**

Gain support within your company

To establish and maintain authority and to achieve success, you will need to gain significant support for your initiatives. Influential, powerful individuals and groups must see it as in their own interests to help you to realise your goals. Do not ignore the politics of organisations, but avoid being thought of as overly 'political'. Political networks—informal bonds, relationships and solidarity among individuals and groups—can either resist your initiatives or help to get things done. Develop contacts and relationships to support your changes. The following actions, taken in sequence, will help you to understand the political processes at work.

1. **Identify opinion leaders.**
2. **Assess their sources of power.**
3. **Identify supporters, opponents and 'undecideds'.**
4. **Analyse interests and develop persuasive arguments.**

Build external support

Success often depends on people you have no direct authority over, including peers and external stakeholders such as customers, suppliers and distributors. The lack of direct authority makes coalition-building with them even more important than it is internally. It is critical to identify your most valuable potential allies and to develop those relationships.

Building external relationships follows the same broad process as internal coalition building. First, identify external players and understand their interests. Consider who is critical to success outside your immediate organisation, within the wider organisation or among external constituencies. It may help you to list the top five individuals or groups and identify their interests and work out where your interests coincide, and where they differ. How can you help to advance goals that are important to them?

Next, understand who within and outside the business has influence and power that can affect your future. How influential are the people loyal to you? Who do you defer to or turn to for advice? Identify the individuals important to your success and the future.

Manage your responses during a downturn, and develop self-awareness

It can be easy to lose your objectivity when the buck stops with you. At times, you may feel that you have to make decisions without all the information you need, and bad decisions are more likely if you lack insights into your own reactions. To guard against this, consider structured self-assessment combined with wise counsel. Set time aside to reflect on what is happening and your reactions, maybe by keeping a daily diary or log. Find time each week to think about how things are going, and consider asking a trusted friend or colleague to help you to analyse the reality of the situation.

The important point is to discipline yourself to review your situation, and then to make sure you take action based on the insights.

There are three potential pitfalls to avoid when assessing your own skills and behaviour.

1. **Regarding a personal failing as a situational problem.**
   Do your difficulties result from your situation, or from
   failures that lie within you? Even experienced, competent
   managers can believe that problems are a result of a
   situation rather than a consequence of their own inaction
   or failures.
2. **Avoiding the new and unfamiliar.** Leaders and managers,
   especially when they are relatively new to a role, are often
   attracted to tasks they feel comfortable with and avoid those
   issues which they are less at home with. Activity is also a
   common form of avoidance. What matters is tackling the right
   issues, not simply acting.
3. **Suppressing doubts and acting with certainty.** A
   frequent response to the demands of a new or challenging
   situation is to suppress doubts in an overly confident manner.
   It is important to project confidence, but the need to appear in
   control can lead you to dismiss opinions, resulting in weak or
   flawed decisions.

- **Set aside 15 minutes at the end or beginning of each week to answer the same set of questions.** If you keep a record of your responses, you can look back and see patterns that develop in the problems you have faced and your typical reactions. This accurate view developed over time will help you to assess the way you lead and your own personal effectiveness.

From time to time, consider how effectively you are working. It can help to focus on four specific areas:

1. **Learning.** How are you learning? Is the balance between technical and leadership learning appropriate? What are your priorities for learning?
2. **Influence.** How well are you influencing key groups, internally and externally? What coalitions do you most need to build?
3. **Execution.** What progress have you made in assessing priorities, opportunities and challenges, and in advancing them?
4. **Self-management.** Have style issues been a problem so far? If so, what can you do about it? Are you using advice effectively?

Build strong leadership at all levels

Five actions will help to develop and maintain leadership at all levels of the organisation during a downturn. They are important disciplines for a firm's survival, promoting commitment and consistency in difficult times.

Empower yourself. Leading people in a downturn means:

- changing your behaviour and highlighting the business's new priorities
- displaying determination and intention
- emphasising competence, initiative and success
- encouraging and enabling people to work in their own way on the priorities you give them

Set a clear vision and challenge. People respond best when they understand what they are doing and why they are doing it. An effective, decisive leader must have the ability to create and communicate a convincing and realistic vision that can be sustained through good times and bad. Not only does it inspire, it also provides a clear focus on a desired outcome, as well as building confidence, teamwork and consistency.

As well as being convincing and realistic, a vision should be powerful if it is to excite and inspire. It should also be specific enough to guide decision-making, and it must be flexible enough to allow for individual initiative as well as changing conditions.

Provide security and support. It is always worth considering contingency measures, but it is important to remain committed to a decision or course. In a downturn, critical decisions are often subject to in-depth analysis and criticism because they matter so much, and any hesitation can quickly cause the decision and its implementation to unravel.

A characteristic of successful leaders is that they provide the people in their organisation with a sense of security and support. If people are to change and grow, a certain level of support is required.

Develop openness. Those who have to lead in difficult circumstances value open and honest discussions based on mutual trust. This matters, because in a downturn customers and employees may think that it is sometimes all right to behave in an unacceptable way. It never is.

Live in balance

Balancing your life and work is important even when things are going well, but during a downturn it'll be invaluable. We all have different ways to guard against stress and combat its effects, but here are some steps you could take:

- **set your own priorities and stick to them**
- **keep your commitments. You'll gain great satisfaction from keeping your word and ticking items off your to-do list.**
- **know yourself. Understand what causes you stress, when you are likely to become stressed and how you can avoid these situations.**
- **take responsibility. Too often people either deny their situation, in which case it will almost certainly worsen, or blame someone (or something) else. Even if it is the fault of someone else, it is you who is being affected and you who needs to resolve it. People are often too afraid to admit that they are suffering from stress, but the longer they put it off, the worse it becomes.**
- **think about what's causing the stress. This can be complicated by the fact that stress is often caused by an accumulation of factors. The solution is to consider**

rationally how to take down the wall that is encircling you, brick by brick. Stress is rarely removed in one leap, but you can tackle it on several fronts.

- anticipate and plan for stressful periods (at work or home). This may include getting temporary resources or people with specific skills to help during a particular period.
- develop strategies for handling stress. What has worked for you in the past? Is there any way you could remove or reduce the cause of the stress, or learn to accept it if it can't be removed?
- relax. This is easier said than done, but the key is to understand that you need to work at relaxing! This may mean planning a holiday or finding a hobby or club that suits you, and then allowing yourself to get absorbed in it. Time away from the causes of stress can help to put the situation in perspective and lead to a new approach that provides a solution.

The dangers of complacency and the art of survival

Having had its problems in the 1970s and 1980s, by 1998 American technology giant Xerox was doing well. A new CEO was in post and there was a rising share price and strong profits. By the end of 1999 significant problems started emerging. There was too much change, too fast; new, opportunistic competitors emerged; economic growth was slowing; and key decisions were flawed. These issues, combined with regulatory issues and cash-flow problems, brought about by a huge fall in revenue, the departure of customers and employees, and debts of US$19 billion.

> 'Good really is the enemy of great—there is no room for complacency.'
>
> Anne Mulcahy

Despite this, Xerox, led by CEO Anne Mulcahy, survived the downturn and staged a remarkable comeback. The business had doubled its share price by 2006, reduced costs by US$2 billion and made profits for the last four years, achieving profits of US$1 billion in 2005.

An improvement in Xerox's business came from a strong brand with a loyal customer base, talented employees, recognition of the need to listen carefully to customers and greater responsiveness. Employees simply wanted a clear direction—no magic, just a focus on sound principles. The key was to win back market share with a competitive range of new products.

Several factors were behind Xerox's resurgence, and these provide a useful guide for executives in other businesses facing similar challenges.

- **Listening and never losing contact. Encourage people to provide constructive criticism and be aware that managers can become out of touch, even within their own organisation.**
- **Improving both costs and service for customers by providing a disciplined way to make improvements.**
- **Recognising the need to be 'problem curious'. Constantly look for ways to be different from your competitors and improve.**

- Providing a clear, exciting and compelling vision of what the future will look like. Remember that in a downturn people value and crave a guiding light and a degree of certainty.
- Investing in the future and innovating. Be prepared to invest. In 2005, two-thirds of Xerox's revenues came from products launched within the last two years.
- Remembering that your business relies on its people and people need to be aligned around a common set of goals and plans Strong leadership is essential; it also means taking great care when you recruit someone that you (and they) are planning for the long-term.

The big lesson from Xerox is that dynamic leadership matters, especially in times of crisis, and often a new, determined and dynamic approach is needed when leading in adversity.

8 LEADING YOUR TEAM DURING TOUGH TIMES

During a time of change, pressure or crisis, problems and conflicts are never far away. In truth, even when the sun is shining and the business is prospering, troubles and conflicts may still be present. The challenge is to find ways to turn a difficult, negative situation into a positive, productive one. In this chapter, we'll look at the factors that can help you do that, including:

■ understanding the causes of conflict
■ techniques for preventing and resolving conflict
■ influencing people
■ leading in difficult times

Understanding the causes of conflict

Conflicts can crop up in any team or work situation but are much more prevalent if the business is struggling. There are many possible causes of conflict, including stress, personality clashes or even bullying behaviour. There are also professional causes of conflict. These might arise from different approaches and ways of working; a fear of change; concern or dissatisfaction with some aspect of employment; or office rumours.

When you own or manage a business, it's likely that you'll be the person called on to sort out these inevitable problems, so think about:

- **when conflicts or disagreements typically arise**
- **who you find yourself in conflict with most often**
- **what issue (or type of issue) generates most heat**

Are there patterns—perhaps particular people, issues or situations around which conflict tends to occur? What lies at the heart of the conflict? How effective are you at resolving it?

Preventing and resolving conflict

Preventing conflict in the first place is, of course, the best way to manage it! Look out for warning signs, such as:

- **team members or colleagues who are always 'too busy'—they're a source of conflict if others have to take on more work as a result**
- **low morale, regular arguments and 'political' difficulties such as gossiping or complaining**
- **a decline in productivity, an increase in mistakes or slipping deadlines**
- **people who are frequently surprised by your actions, what you are doing and what you expect of them—they obviously aren't tuned in to what the team needs to be concentrating on**
- **colleagues who put off doing tasks or keep asking for your advice and help without at least trying to solve a problem themselves**

- an increase in worrying comments from others, such as customers, your boss or other people in the organisation
- team members questioning their role, worrying, complaining or leaving

This is, of course, by no means an exhaustive list, but you can clearly see the type of signs that would indicate that things aren't going well. Similar problems will probably occur from time to time anyway, but what matters is how often they arise and how long they lurk.

Prevent conflict

Sorting out tense situations and relationships can soak up a great deal of time, so nip it in the bud by:

- making sure everyone in the business is communicating openly and honestly. By maintaining a dialogue, you will be able to spot conflicts and resentments building up.
- assessing the culture and management style of your team or business. Is it too aggressive? Is there an atmosphere of intense competition, rivalry or blame? Is it conservative? Are some people obsessed with their job titles? While it's unrealistic to expect that you'll be able to change the culture of the company *completely*, encourage others to make allowances and build the best team possible to meet your goals. Building team spirit helps to prevent ill feeling. If you can instil a sense of common purpose, it's likely that you'll reduce the chances of conflict.

- making people aware of what behaviour is acceptable and what is not, as early as possible: be clear about what you're expecting from new employees when you go through the recruitment process, for example. Also set a good example yourself: your team will watch how you work, how you treat people and how you approach business situations. Match your leadership style to the tasks that you need to accomplish and the team that you're leading.
- showing that you're approachable. Hiding in your office during trying times won't promote an effective, harmonious team. If people feel able to discuss situations with you, potential problems will be defused before they get out of hand.

When conflict arises, there are several approaches you can adopt. There is no single way to resolve conflicts, of course, because they can vary so widely, but there are some approaches that are widely used by successful leaders.

- **Talk to each person individually.** Try to remain neutral, objective and constructive, even if the people involved are trying your patience. Encourage each person to express their grievances clearly and specifically: often when people are upset and under stress they can feel overwhelmed and feel that *everyone* is getting at them *all* the time. Draw out information about specific issues that you can tackle together. It's also useful to ask the parties involved how they would like to see the issue resolved: they will then feel that they 'own' the solution more. Having said that, if you reach an impasse, you may need to decide the best course of action yourself. If this is the case, keep calm and explain why you've chosen this course of action.

- **Make the parties to the conflict face their situation and communicate.** If you get too involved in the detail and complexity of the conflict, your authority and ability to resolve the issue may be undermined. The parties to the conflict need to understand that it is their responsibility and that they need to help to resolve it: clear, regular, open communication is a good first step.

- **Make the parties work together.** It may be that the problem could be resolved if each person understood the other person better. It may also be that there is no other alternative: they will have to get on; so get them to realise the fact quickly.

Manage reactions and handle disagreements

If you're directly involved with one side of a conflict, there are several ways to manage the situation. (These may be particularly useful if you're giving feedback to someone in a performance appraisal or project meeting.) The key is to be aware of the need to manage reactions and handle disagreements.

Maintain trust

Make sure that you avoid rumours, misunderstandings and unnecessary complications by keeping confidentiality, especially with sensitive personnel issues. Being critically aware when communicating requires a variety of skills, in particular:

- **reacting to ideas, not to people**
- **focusing on the significance of the facts and evidence**

■ avoiding jumping to conclusions

■ listening for how things are said and what is *not* said

When you're talking to someone, be aware of their concerns and reactions, and to do this you need to create an environment where they can be honest and open. Even then, some people will still not say how they feel or what they think, or they may simply lack the skills to express themselves adequately. In these circumstances, ask open, probing questions that will provide an indication of what the person is thinking, such as, 'How do you feel about that?', or 'What's your initial reaction?'.

Allow managers greater latitude

Leadership can often be a lonely activity, and shutting people out can make it even lonelier both for you and for them. Again, the extent to which you grant freedom and latitude depends on your own leadership style, but letting people do some or all of the following will help to bring out their best. Consider allowing them to:

■ **follow up their own initiatives and ideas, without necessarily consulting you (or set parameters where they do not have to consult)**

■ **decide how they will pursue their own professional development**

■ **manage their own resources, particularly staff and money**

■ **make mistakes in a blame-free environment**

■ **challenge you on anything you do that affects their work**

- manage their work environment
- develop their individual leadership style
- take the lead in monitoring and reviewing their performance
- know that you support them

Leading in adversity
Be resilient

Resilience is the ability to keep things together during times of enormous stress and change. More than education, experience or training, how resilient you are will determine who succeeds and fails. Research suggests that three fundamental characteristics set resilient people and companies apart from others:

1. the capacity to face reality, rather than ignore it
2. the ability to understand why something has happened, and find something positive wherever possible—this can sustain morale through the troubling times of a downturn
3. the ability to improvise and be flexible—this is valuable at any time, but especially so during a downturn

Dos and don'ts: leading in tough times
Do

- back up other leaders' decisions when they need support in front of others, even if you don't agree with them completely
- provide active support by guiding, coaching and counselling—these are far more effective than criticism, negativity or disagreement

- be clear about your expectations and share these with colleagues
- be honest and open—if you hide information or your own mistakes, even inadvertently, you can cause mistrust or resentment; share information with colleagues so they can do their job
- examine assumptions. If someone succeeds or fails, is it the result of what they did or how they did it? If they are reluctant or concerned, is it for a reason you understand, or could it be because of something else?

Don't

- Manipulate people with implied rewards ('if you do X, you'll get a bonus) or guilt-trip them into doing something: show respect and build trust.
- Dwell on mistakes; people usually realise when they have made a mistake and you should always try to give the person the opportunity to correct it.
- Undermine people. This is an important rule at any time and never more so than when handling challenges and influencing people; agree clear guidelines for monitoring progress and then stick to them.
- Rush: you will make mistakes.

Improve listening and empathy

- Keep a notebook and get into the habit of noting down key points during discussions and meetings. This is a journalistic skill; as well as providing a valuable record for future reference, it will also train you to listen 'actively' (see below).

- Develop your knowledge, understanding and use of body language. Understanding non-verbal communication is a valuable way to uncover how people feel as well as what they think about an issue.
- Think about how others might react or behave in a specific situation (Do this in advance of a meeting, negotiation or discussion).

Decisiveness is vital for influencing people, as well as for preventing or resolving conflict. Once you have assessed your position, you need to choose the best option and then take action. Ask yourself:

- What are you going to do?
- When are you going to do it?
- Who needs to know?
- What support and resources do you need and how will you get them?
- How will the above help you to achieve your goals?
- What obstacles might hinder you and what strategies would counter them?

Business downturns increase the number of decisions that need to be made. However, don't wait for a downturn to hit before you flex your decision-making muscles! If you have to learn in the middle of a problem, the process will become complex, distracted and overly experimental, making it harder to succeed. Turn to the next chapter for more advice on how to make the process a success and avoid some of the pitfalls along the way.

A practical guide to leading in turbulent times

What are the lessons from one of severest recessions in history—the global downturn and financial crisis that began in developed economies in 2008?

First, **leadership is a journey, not a destination**. This has several significant implications for leaders: notably the need to be flexible, self-aware, tireless and dynamic. Turbulent times provide leaders with an opportunity to develop and improve their skills in several important areas.

- **Discovery and risk.** When you think you're leading at your best what is it that you're doing? Questioning is a valuable skill that leads to improved understanding, creativity and risk management. During a downturn, there is a danger that leaders can be controlling and dismiss any thought of empowerment. This is often because they are concerned about the need to control their environment and situation. What is needed is the opposite: recognition that, when combined with sound leadership, issues such as empowerment and an ability to prosper from risk are sources of strength and opportunity.

- **Purpose and meaning** is another area where the role and impact of the leader is vital. During a downturn, it is especially important for people to perform at their best, working productively and effectively. The danger, however, is that 'people' issues are dismissed or rejected as a low priority—desirable but not essential. In fact, the opposite is true. People are personally concerned about their welfare during a downturn; they need reassurance and confidence that the business is moving determinedly in the right direction. People work better when their efforts have purpose and meaning, and these are best uncovered by each individual—they cannot simply be bestowed by someone else. The leader's task, therefore, is to help guide people so they can recognise the value and contribution they are making. This then results in a level of engagement, confidence and success that is an asset to the business rather than a potential weakness.

- **Shared vision and clear focus** are also important; with leaders needing to help people stay engaged with the challenges of the business and channel their energies in the right direction.

- **Maintaining standards of ethical behaviour** is also an essential task for leaders during a downturn. This can be notoriously difficult to accomplish but leaders can make progress by: acting as a role model and showing the standards required; providing clear and explicit communications; understanding where the biggest risks may lie—don't ignore concerns, and getting the right people to do the work, and recognising that if people are unsure or pressured they may cut corners.

- **Intuitive thinking** is also something that the leader needs to develop—both for themselves and in others. Making a decision and implementing it can be very messy. No matter how much planning and preparation takes place, the process is often confusing, fast moving and uncertain—and therefore tense and unsettling. It is comforting to think of decision making as a rational, methodical and ordered process, but the reality is different. Events are not always ordered or clear and the relevant information may be unavailable, making it more difficult to classify, define, specify and arrive at a decision that will be effective. An intuitive approach provides the inspiration and insight needed to identify and explore the best options.

- **Connection and authenticity** are also important leadership traits. This means being yourself, even during times of pressure or stress. It relies on leaders having a strong belief in their skills and ability and expressing themselves as they are, rather than trying to be something they are not.

- **Intention** is always important, and never more than during a downturn. Leaders need to demonstrate a positive, helpful intention in their interactions with others and a real desire to connect.

- **Discipline and humility** are also perennially important and assume special significance during a recession. The ability for a leader to set aside their ego and identify and to persist with the most important challenges, and then provide practical support to others, is essential for success.

Frequently-asked questions

Do the priorities for leaders change in a long-term crisis?

No, these characteristics of leadership are timeless and consistent and they also apply across cultures. An interesting aspect of leadership during a recession is the opportunity to do something that may seem paradoxical or counter-intuitive. For example, train people that you were thinking of making redundant. They are likely to respond positively, with renewed commitment, with the result that redundancy is unnecessary.

Which issues are most important?

Each issue is significant for different people and in different circumstances. Not everyone is capable of leading—what matters is finding people with the innate character and desire to lead.

How significant is communication for leaders during turbulent times?

It is vital for several reasons. During periods of uncertainty, or when situations are fluid and changeable, people need:

- **to understand the direction or vision for their work—something to guide their thinking and focus their efforts**
- **to be able to give and receive information and contribute to the way that decisions are made and implemented**
- **to possess the clarity and confidence that comes from open communications**

Action Checklist: Creating a resilient organisation that can adapt and survive

- **Remember that well-run businesses don't react hastily** to economic news or even their own specific challenges—the best businesses take a careful, measured approach that accurately reflects their situation and priorities.

- **Personal responsibility and accountability are essential.** Leaders need to avoid the blame game, lead by example and encourage their colleagues to seize the initiative.
- **Be nimble.** Those businesses that will succeed (now and in the future) are flexible and able to adapt. New markets and even new product developments can continue to provide some firms with new opportunities.
- **Remember that people are capable of amazing things, even during a recession.** In fact, the pressures exerted during a downturn may result in greater ingenuity, productivity and innovation. However, this requires a progressive approach and the ability to break with the past. Some people can achieve this, others cannot.
- **If costs are fixed, you need to sell your way out of trouble,** possibly by changing the business model.
- **Courage, openness and honesty are invaluable.** They draw people together and provide opportunities to improve the business. Tenacity is also important. Collaboration and a supportive approach are also important ways to encourage innovation.
- **If redundancy is unavoidable, then a clear process is essential.** Respect and support for people that have to leave the business are important for credibility and morale and to avoid unintended consequences.
- **Recognize** the four ways that organisations can 'get stuck' and fail to break free from a downturn:

1. genuinely trying harder with the actions of the past, instead of seeking a new approach, convinced that greater effort is the key to success
2. implementing 'if only' solutions—terrible over-simplifications that can often result from a desire to shift the blame onto others
3. pursuing 'utopian' solutions to challenges that are past or irrelevant—for example, implementing BPR (business process reengineering) when the biggest challenge does not lie in the business's processes
4. getting trapped in paradoxes—for example, screaming at people to 'Take the initiative!' and then wondering why they seem reluctant to do so . . .

■ **Engage with people informally.** Rigid change management methods will not result in transformation—this arises informally.

■ **Break free from conventional thinking when stuck with a problem,** known solutions can often simply reinforce it. This can be achieved by involving people at all levels of the business and asking the miracle question: what if?

■ **Provide provocative leadership.** Disturbing the status quo is a useful way to keep people fresh, forward-thinking and dynamic.

■ **Embrace difference as a source of potential advantage** and an opportunity to learn. Combined with this is an ability to 'Say yes to the mess!' Be tolerant of other people's ideas and activities; support them and build on their ideas.

- **Minimise organisational structure and hierarchy** as a way of encouraging innovation; instead, give people a broad direction and the opportunity to take their own path.
- **Understand the need for situational leadership** and balance the needs of the task, team and individual and that responds to each specific set of circumstances.

MAKING DECISIONS AND SOLVING PROBLEMS

Surviving a downturn involves making key business decisions and solving problems, often under pressure. If you're feeling low, sometimes you may want to put off taking decisions because you can't see the point of them, but being proactive and motivated is (as we saw in Chapter 1) a key way to get the business back on its feet.

Mastering decision making

During a downturn, with slashed margins and a competitive market, it's important to keep your head and to use a methodical process for decisions, even if you feel a bit panicky.

Balance 'rational' and 'intuitive' decision-making

When making decisions and solving problems rationally—that is, without the benefit of more intuitive techniques that build on your instinct, experiences and 'gut' feeling—it's important to be aware of the major steps that form the decision-making process.

■ **Assessing the situation.** Start by asking whether the decision relates to a permanent, underlying or structural issue, or whether it is the result of a one-off event. Some decisions are generic and are best addressed with a consistent rule or principle, whereas others are best resolved when they arise. Having said that, what may appear to be an isolated event is often an early indicator of a generic problem.

- **Defining the critical issues.** The critical issues to consider include understanding who is affected, likely developments, the timescale involved and sensitive issues, as well as previous, comparable situations. The key is to focus on *all* of the relevant issues: a partial analysis is almost as bad as no analysis at all, as it gives an ill-founded over-confidence in the decision. 'Funnelling' is a useful technique to use; it involves collecting as much information and data as possible and prioritising and eliminating themes to clarify a few, critical issues.

- **Clearly define what the decision needs to achieve.** Every decision should have a minimum set of goals: rules to comply with, a timescale for completion and a method of execution. Working through these issues means that you'll be able to implement your final decision and actually make something happen. Potential conflicts need to be clearly understood, monitored and, where necessary, resolved.

- **Making the decision.** Decisions often involve compromise—sometimes the ideal solution just isn't attainable. Always have a clear view of the 'ideal' decision, then test it, and, if compromise is necessary, make sure it is made positively, with a clear focus remaining on what needs to be achieved.

- **Implementing the decision.** Executing the decision is usually the most time-consuming and critical phase. It means understanding the activities that will be required and clearly assigning responsibility for individual tasks. You'll also have to communicate with the right people and manage resources, so that the people carrying out the decision have everything they need to complete their task.

- **Keeping an eye on things and adjusting as necessary.** There are two certainties in decision-making: first, the people who make and implement decisions are fallible; second, the context in which decisions are taken will probably change. As a result, you'll need to keep a close eye on the implementation so that you can tweak the next steps as necessary. Make sure that you're visible and that your team knows that they can come to you with any queries. Don't hide in your office and wait to be brought bad news: there's no substitute for walking about the office, shop or factory to see how things are going and to make sure that disaster isn't imminent.

Incorporating intuition

It is comforting to think of decision-making as a rational, methodical and ordered process, but the reality is different. It can be messy. No matter how much planning and preparation takes place, the process is often confusing, fast moving and uncertain. Events aren't always clear and the relevant information may not always be ready when you need it, which means that it can be difficult to arrive at an effective decision. The intuitive approach can act as a counterpoint to the rational approach discussed above and can provide the inspiration, insight and instinct that are needed to identify and explore the best options.

To make intuition work, remember that:

- **instinct and intuition are valuable forms of unspoken knowledge.** Our minds are continuously processing information subconsciously. Intuition is a form of 'unspoken' knowledge that complements rather than undermines the rational approach to decision-making.
- **emotions 'filter' and guide our decisions.** Decisions are guided by our emotions that act as filters, prioritising information and provoking a physical response to influences, from laughter to stress. Make sure that you know how to manage emotion and instinct effectively, as they provide a powerful means to produce insight and they influence behaviour in solving problems.
- **instinct and pattern recognition can provide the key to analysis and creativity.** Effective analysis depends upon seeing the links between various data and then interpreting the patterns. The ability to perceive patterns across issues, data and subjects is what separates exceptional decision-makers from good ones.

Avoiding the pitfalls of decision-making

Unfortunately, during downturns decisions and solutions to problems fail with at least the same frequency as they do during better times. Knowing where, when, how and why decisions usually fail is essential to ensuring that your decisions don't. Some common pitfalls can include the following.

Paralysis by analysis

Common in many organisations, this happens when people analyse and discuss an issue for too long when they should, in fact, be doing something about it. It can happen because people become obsessed with monitoring the situation, understanding how widespread an issue is and constantly focusing on defensive measures. All of these are, of course, useful at the right time, but at the wrong time they can make things worse: if you're drowning, it doesn't help to measure the depth of the water!

> Decision-makers need to be aware of the consequences of delay and possess the courage to decide. This is never more vital than during a downturn.

The 'knowing–doing' gap

This concept is similar to paralysis by analysis, except the emphasis is less on finding out what has happened and much more on finding solutions, discussing options, planning the best approach . . . but not ever actually carrying out any of the solutions. In short: you know what you should be doing, but never actually do it!

Ignorance and mistakes

With paralysis by analysis and the knowing-doing gap, people are aware that things aren't right and that they're working to improve them. There is at least a chance of success and the possibility that things will improve. More often, however, businesses don't even get that far: although they have available the necessary information, they're either complacent or just don't see the signs.

Information overload

The technological developments we all benefit from today mean that information is never in short supply. However, what can be hard is separating the wheat from the chaff: we receive so much data that relevant and important details can be obscured, making decision-making harder in the process. The solution is to be clear about what information you need, when and why, and then use this to help you make the best decisions.

Avoiding the pitfalls in decision-making and problem-solving

We all make mistakes from time to time, but being actively aware of some of the pitfalls that we can encounter will save you time and money in the long run.

For example, look out for:

- the failure to define and understand the problem or decision in the first place
- subjective, irrational analysis, which includes prejudice or being unduly influenced by your own personal feelings or perceptions; objective, unbiased analysis is best
- insensitivity: anticipate problems and the effects their solutions will bring
- lack of focus: don't let problem-solving become hampered by a lack of clear objectives or priorities
- lack of creativity and innovation: don't always rely on experience or past approaches, even when they're

tried and tested. They may not be effective in every single case and certain problems may need a completely new method to solve them.

- hasty and inappropriate action: under the guise of being decisive, it is often tempting to act without properly considering the best solution; this is further complicated when some situations require quick decisions, and knowing which approach fits each situation is important for success
- over-confidence: sometimes the solution may seem obvious, but a better solution may lie hidden elsewhere. Be open to alternative solutions (proposed by other people!).
- too much aversion to risk: in a downturn, you need to be ready and willing to take calculated risks. Hesitation and fear of failure may be natural, but you need to show the way in controlling risk and managing the situation

Problem-solving under pressure

Surviving a downturn means solving problems. Problems crop up more frequently in a downturn and may result from new issues—such as reduced sales revenues, fiercer competition and higher interest rates—or from a heightening of existing issues, such as the increased need to maintain product quality when faced with more demanding customers. The extra pressure of the downturn forces people to focus on improving the way that they solve problems and how they perceive, recognise and react to problems. Solving problems under pressure is about remaining calm and focused, without letting other issues cloud your judgement.

As with decision-making, problem-solving during stressful times requires action and development both during the downturn and during more comfortable times. This is so that you develop the best way of recognising and dealing with problems for you.

Problem-solving is a central aspect of leadership: it distinguishes a maintenance manager (someone who preserves the status quo) from a visionary leader, someone who can anticipate and prevent problems, or even turn a problem into an opportunity. As with making decisions, solving problems effectively involves getting to the heart of matter quickly—and then doing something about it!

Understanding the problem

Doctors observe the symptoms of an illness to try to establish the cause and decide what treatment to prescribe. When you need to solve a problem, using a 'cause and effect' analysis will help you work out how best to treat the issues facing your business. It involves working out the effects of the problem in order to determine what the actual problem is and how to deal with it.

This powerful technique requires you to:

- label the problem
- identify its root causes
- collect data on the causes

Cause and effect analysis is one technique of using an understanding of the problem so that you can work out the best solution. To understand a problem, though, it is best to have an understanding of how problems usually emerge and you need to know how to distinguish between different types of problem.

It is important to understand whether frequently recurring problems are, in reality, several completely different problems: Pareto analysis can be useful in organising the data so that the most significant factors influencing the problems are clearly illustrated. This method is based upon the 80–20 Pareto principle: namely that 80% of problems are caused by 20% of possible factors. Therefore, assessing the trouble-making 20% is necessary. The four steps in Pareto analysis are:

1. **identifying the main problem**
2. **determining the factors causing it and how they do this**
3. **listing the biggest factors contributing to the problem; Pareto analysis is most useful when relatively few factors are involved**
4. **developing a solution targeting each factor individually**

This approach has the potential to eliminate the major causes of a problem, which often prevents it recurring or mitigates its effects. But it is less useful when a large number of factors are more or less equally responsible, as it's difficult and time-consuming to treat each one and pointless to prioritise the order that they are dealt with. The more complicated the problem, the less likely it is that Pareto analysis will help to find a solution. For complex problems, creative problem-solving is required.

Applying the right problem-solving technique

Having understood what the causes and effects of a problem are, you need to solve it. Creatively solving a problem and implementing it can be harder than understanding it, but the following techniques help.

Overcome barriers. The first step in solving a problem is often to recognise that one exists; while this may appear obvious, it is often overlooked.

To overcome barriers you need to:

- recognise the cause of the problem
- create an environment where problems are openly acknowledged and discussed
- create an environment that pre-empts difficulties before they arise
- define the problem: ask what, when, where and who? Remember what you are trying to achieve with a solution and clearly communicate this to all involved in problem-solving. Sometimes unplanned and unwelcome events occur, but they may not necessarily be *problems*. If they do not cause ongoing difficulties, or, if nothing can be done about them, then, in certain instances, consider pressing on without attempting any 'corrective' action.

Identify potential solutions. Remember that you're not only treating the symptoms, you also need to tackle the causes of the problem. These causes can impact on other areas; it is worth considering how the solution to one problem affects other parts of the organisation. One technique for finding the best solution is brainstorming. Gathering as many ideas together as possible that might solve the problem or form a part of the solution, and then assessing each idea, seeing how practical it is, where it links with other ideas and whether it could provide the answer.

Check the solution. Imagine how the solution will work in practice and where it might fail and adjust it if necessary. You should also:

- remember first principles
- assess the likely consequences of the solution
- consider additional solutions and actions

Make the decision. Select the most promising solution and plan its implementation. Common dangers at this point include:

- **procrastination and decision avoidance**
- **paralysis by analysis**
- **mismanaging risk**
- **disregarding intuition and experience**
- **lacking confidence**

Monitor the results. Monitoring the effects of the solution enables adjustments to be made. Even if the solution is not the best one, it may still lead to the desired result with careful monitoring and some remedial action.

A final thought: surviving a downturn

For your business to survive a downturn, it (and you) have to be ready to change and adapt those things that need to improve, while also recognising and keeping hold of the best of the past. In doing this, several perennial techniques are valuable, notably the ability to display assertive, dynamic leadership that changes and improves the way people work.

A strategy, however brilliant, will fail unless your people are emotionally committed to it. You have to sell it to them, showing dynamic leadership.

Too often, people's day-to-day behaviour actually undermines the ability to survive a downturn. You and colleagues in your business may be unhappy, concerned, hesitant, or just faced with a choice between 'less worse' options.

Several factors can help to avoid this and improve your ability to survive a downturn. First, start with the people and attitude within your business. Both need to be positive, with people understanding the best way forward.

Values are also significant: don't expect people to do things that are contrary to their values. Phrase requests and challenges in ways that appeal to people's values and priorities. When surviving a downturn, a questioning approach is also valuable, as well as a willingness to experiment, to learn and to tolerate mistakes. Finally, personal responsibility, direction and leadership are vital.

Above all, remember that the starting place for surviving a downturn is to understand that the solution lies within you; take action in the most important areas and always work to learn and improve. If that happens, everything else will follow.

INDEX

A

acid test ratio 35–6
advance payments/deposits
   113
adversity, leading in 149
authenticity 154
average cost pricing 80
awareness, increasing 37

B

balance, living in 139–40
barrier pricing 81
barriers, overcoming 167–8
believing in yourself 4–5
Black Swan events 22
boosting profitability 25–53
break-even analysis 75
budgets 111, 116
building rapport 95 0, 101,
   102–3
'business as usual' thinking
   9–10
business ideas
   factors 11–12
   getting the right 12–13
business relationships,
   developing 18–20
buyer's cycle 89–91

C

cash 20–1
cash flow
   controlling 109–21
   forecast 117–21
cash management 14, 50–1
'cause and effect' analysis
   166–7
causes of downturns 1–24
change, leading 127–9
colleagues, relationships with
   19–20
commercial awareness 7–8
commercial opportunities 51
communication 155
competition 11–12
competitors
   awareness of 56–7
   recognising your 74
   staying ahead of 57
   understanding 72
complacency 8–10, 140–2
complaining 6–7
conflict
   preventing and resolving
      144–7
   understanding causes of
      143–4

confrontation 130
connection 154
contacts, developing 95–6
corporate visions 125–7
costs
    awareness of 115–16
    controlling 48–50,
        109–21
    fixed 156
    reasons for rising 111
    reviewing 74–5
cost-volume-profit (CVP)
    analysis 75
courage 156
creativity 15–17
credibility 134
credit limits 113
creditors
    average payment period 35
    managing 115
credit references 112–13
current ratio 35
customary pricing 80–1
customers
    feedback from 59–60,
        85–6
    focusing on 17–18, 54–67
    gaining trust of 87
    identifying profitable
        60, 85
    making it easy for 100–1

managing issues with 49–50
perceptions and behaviour
    73–4
relationships with 15, 66–7
understanding 64, 71–2,
    88–9

D

database marketing 82–3
debtors 35
decision-making 155, 159–65
decisiveness 151–2
dependability 133
deposits 113
direct mail marketing 82–3
direct selling 82
disagreements 147
discipline 154
diversification 38, 43–4
downturns
    causes of 1–24
    leading businesses through
        122–42
    recognising 22–4

E

EasyJet 16–17
emotions 162
empathy 150–1
empowerment 152
engagement 157

entrepreneurial ability 36–8
ethical behaviour 153

F
fact-finding 104–5
failure 3
financial controls 11
Flandro, Gary 2–3

G
General Electric (GE) 29–30
goal setting 5–6
gross profit 34
guiding coalition 127–8
guiding visions 123–4, 125–6

H
honesty 156
horizontal integration 42–3
hygiene factors 11–12, 14–15

I
ignorance 163–4
information 8–9, 164
innovation 15–17, 131–2
insight 2–3
inspiration 2–3
instinct 162
integration 38, 42–3
intention 154
internet selling 83

intuition 153–4, 159–62
intuitive decision-making
    159–62
invoicing 111–12
IT systems 56

J
just-in-time (JIT) production
    114

K
key performance indicators
    106, 110
'knowing-doing' gap 163
knowledge, using 8–9

L
late payments 113–14
leadership
    leading change 127–9
    through a downturn 122–42
    in times of change 132–40
    trustworthy 129–32
    during tough times 143–58
learning organisation 9
listening 150–1
loss leading 76–7

M
management style, poor 14
marginal cost pricing 79

market demand 11
marketing 34, 70–2
market research 55
market segmentation 65–6, 71
market sensing 65
market share 34–5
MATE model 93–4
measurement 46
mergers and acquisitions
    (M&As) 38, 39–42
milking 77–8
mindset 4–7
mistakes 163–4
moral courage 133
moral hazard 21–2

N
NASA 2
Nespresso 26–8
net profit 34

O
objections, handling 100
organic growth 38, 39
organisational structure 158
overheads 117

P
paralysis by analysis 163
payments, receiving prompt
    112

penetration pricing 77
people issues 152–3
price differentiation 78–9
price/earnings (P/E) ratio 36
price innovations 48
pricing 72–3
pricing strategy 76–81
problem-solving 164–9
production management 49
products
    boosting profitability of
        45–8
    developing 30–2, 66
    knowledge and
        differentiation 71
    managing least profitable
        33
    problems with 7
profitability 25–53
provocative leadership 157
purchasing, managing 115

Q
quality 49, 116
quick ratio 35–6

R
rapport 95–6, 101, 102–3
ratio analysis 33–6
rational decision-making
    159–62

redundancy 156
relationships 18–20, 95–6
resilience 149
responses 3–4, 135–7
responsibility, taking 3–4
revenue, increasing 68–87
Richer, Julian 20
risk management 152
risks, reducing 49
rule of five 6
rules of engagement 20

S
sales
   improving 88–108
   increasing 69–70
   monitoring 49–50
sales growth 34
sales meetings 101–6
sales proposals 47–8, 96–100
sales revenue, increasing 46–8
sales techniques 82–7
savings, finding 110–11
self-awareness 135–7
self-confidence 37
shareholders 15
Sharpbenders' research 10–11,
   13–14
short-term wins 129
skills, developing 51–2
skimming 77–8

Sobal-Nespresso 27–8
specialisation 38, 44–5
special offers 83
stakeholders 15
statement of purpose 104
stock levels 114–15
stock turnover 35
strategic position 25–6
strategic selling 92–5
strategies 13, 25–9, 128
success 2–3
suppliers 15, 49
support 134–5
survival, art of 140–2

T
Taleb, Nassim Nicholas 22
target pricing 79
team sales performance,
   improving 106–8
trust 131–3, 147–8
trustworthy leadership 129–32

U
uniqueness 12
unique sales objective 92–3
unique sales point (USP) 101

V
value of work in hand 34
variable pricing 79–80

vertical integration
42–3
visions 6, 38
developing 128
establishing compelling
122–5
establishing corporate
125–7

shared 153
understanding of 155

W

wastage 116–17

X

Xerox 10, 47, 140–2